The We... Whistleblowers

The Westminster Whistleblowers

Shirley Porter, homes for votes and twenty years of scandal in Britain's rottenest borough

Paul Dimoldenberg

POLITICO'S

First published in Great Britain 2006 by
Politico's Publishing Ltd, an imprint of
Methuen Publishing Ltd
11–12 Buckingham Gate
London
SW1E 6LB

10 9 8 7 6 5 4 3 2 1

A CIP catalogue record for this book is available from the British Library.

ISBN-10: 1-84275-179-4
ISBN-13: 978-1-84275-179-4

Typeset by SX Composing DTP, Rayleigh, Essex
Printed and bound in Great Britain by Cromwell Press Ltd, Trowbridge,
Wiltshire

Contents

Dedicated to the memory of Vincent Allan, Hugh Garside, Joe Glickman, George Lowe, Jean Merriton, Jill Selbourne and John Thirlwell, Westminster Labour Councillors with whom I have been proud to serve and who are sadly no longer with us.

'For more than fifteen years a small group of activists have untiringly sustained the pressure to bring the culprits of the gerrymandering to account. As a result, all councillors and senior officials know that they cannot act in this way, and the probity of local government has been upheld.

'When faced with abuse and malpractice, with the odds stacked against stopping it, the temptation to say "nothing can be done" is very strong. The Westminster Objectors show us all that, in fact, something can be done.'

Chris Holmes, former director of Shelter, *Housing Today*,
4 June 2004

'This is about the wholesale corruption of a council, the ruthless and systematic subversion of a locally elected bureaucracy under its leader, Lady Porter, to service the interests of the Conservative Party.'

Melanie Phillips, *Observer*, 13 November 1994

Acknowledgements

I began writing this account of the last twenty years when preparing my defence of the Standards Board for England's charges against me. In its raw format it was a straightforward 'chronology' of events, which drew extensively on district auditor John Magill's 1994 and 1996 reports and the various High Court, Court of Appeal and House of Lords 'Homes for Votes' judgments.

I have also quoted from internal Westminster City Council documents, some of which were made available to me under the Freedom of Information Act and others which I acquired through questions and inquiries.

In particular, I owe a great debt of gratitude to Jonathan Rosenberg, who helped me to amass a huge collection of relevant papers, and to Veronica Mockler, secretary to successive leaders of the opposition, for the way in which she managed to ferret out the most obscure documents and reports.

After years of being told by the Conservatives that the 'Homes for Votes' story was 'ancient history' and of no interest to anyone in the twenty-first century, I was apprehensive when first asking a few close friends to read the draft manuscript. Thankfully, Roger Davenport, Janice and Herman Kok, Rupert D'Cruz, Joe Hegarty, David Pitt-Watson, Peter Bradley and Richard Holmes reassured me that there was a story of interest to tell. I am grateful to all of them for their confidence and helpful comments.

Similar thanks are due to my agent, Jeffrey Simmons, for his support and words of wisdom, and also to Alan Gordon Walker and Jonathan Wadman at Politico's.

Finally, I could not have done anything without the love and support of Linda, Amelia and Zoe.

Introduction

As I walked out of the Aeonian Centre, just off Tottenham Court Road, into the sunlight, at 4.30 p.m. on Friday 20 May 2005, it was as if a massive weight had been lifted from my shoulders. For almost two years I had been under investigation by the local government watchdog, the Standards Board for England. My 'crime' was to pass confidential information to the BBC about Westminster City Council's failure to take effective action to recover the £42 million surcharge owed by the Council's former leader, Dame Shirley Porter, for her part in the notorious 'Homes for Votes' scandal of the late 1980s. I faced disqualification or suspension from the Council for up to five years, if found guilty.

For over twenty years Labour councillors had been a constant thorn in the side of Westminster Conservatives. Despite their large majority, as the scandals mounted the Conservatives were reduced to the laughing stock of local government. And that was no accident. Every time they blundered we made sure that people knew about it. The list of scandals grew month by month. And Shirley Porter's 'Homes for Votes' was top of the pile.

Shirley Porter's Westminster was a place of fear. She rode roughshod over her Conservative Party colleagues and Council staff. Those who opposed her were either sacked or rendered 'politically dead'. The only people who stood up to her were Labour councillors and a number of determined local residents' groups. The daughter of Tesco founder Jack Cohen, she was used to having her own way. 'What Shirley wants Shirley gets' summed up her approach to life and to dealing with people. If it worked in business for her father, then why shouldn't it work in local politics, too?

Some say that Porter only went into politics because, although her father was her role-model, Jack Cohen never saw either of his two daughters as his business heir. She took this badly and she never forgave her father's eventual successor, Ian MacLaurin, for taking what she believed was rightfully hers. After thwarting Porter's attempts to gain a seat on the Tesco board in the 1980s, MacLaurin later admitted: 'I may share some responsibility for what happened later at Westminster City Council, though there is some consolation in the fact that, if she hadn't ruined the City's reputation, she would have ruined Tesco instead' (*Independent*, 25 March 2005).

Local government had never seen anything like Shirley Porter. Her 'mission' drove a relentless and manic whirlwind of activity as she prowled the streets recording into her Dictaphone details of overflowing litter bins and broken street lights, which she expected Council officials to have fixed by the end of the day. Days after her election as Council leader in 1983, she wrote to every member of staff 'to warn the lazy and inefficient to be on their guard'. Making a very definite break with the past, she argued that past Conservative leaders 'didn't understand the commercial, sordid side of life'. She was also the first – and last – Council leader to turn up at City Hall in a pink tracksuit.

But it was her belief that she was 'always right' that marked her out from other Council leaders. Most seasoned politicians take 'the rough with the smooth'. Sometimes the political tide is with you. At other times, no matter what you do, the voters insist on voting for others. But Porter's arrogance did not tolerate any 'give and take'. She wanted it all, all the time. So when, after Labour came so close to winning the Council at the 1986 elections, the Conservatives looked down the jaws of a possible electoral defeat in 1990, Porter's response was to believe that she had the right to move Conservative voters into and Labour voters out of Westminster to get the election result she wanted.

It was the same when it came to taking professional advice from Council staff. If Council officers advised caution in taking up her latest cost-cutting exercise, it was seen as 'being negative'. It was in this climate that the 15p sale of the Council's three cemeteries took place. There was an arrogance about Porter's politics, which blocked out anything that got in the way of her objective.

The heartless and incompetent sale of the Westminster cemeteries shocked people all over the country. Porter's insensitivity and total disregard for people's feelings were summed up by her reaction to the 'fuss'. 'They were an expensive liability. It's the mowing round the headstones, that costs money. I even went to the Garden of Rest at Los Angeles to see their flat headstones,' she claimed in 1988. Later, she revealed: 'I remember all these discussions about how beautiful it was and we certainly said, "Look, this is ridiculous."'

To this day, I doubt if she understands the deep feelings of anger that were stirred up among the relatives of those buried in the three cemeteries. She was always right. Anyone else's feelings, for whatever reason, had little value or relevance to her.

And, of course, the arrogance that was to prove Porter's downfall was the fatal decision to leave a 'paper-trail' of all the 'Homes for Votes' meetings: discussions, reports, charts, tables, minutes and notes. The masses of paper later uncovered by district auditor John Magill sealed her fate. What she and her colleagues did was all written down in detail. The names, the dates and the unlawful decisions were all there in black and white.

This was unique in local government history. Even though local government in Britain is no stranger to scandal – remember Poulson in the 1960s, Lambeth and Hackney in the 1980s and Doncaster in the 1990s – Porter's Westminster set a new standard. In the 1980s there were in some places vague rumours that Wandsworth's new Conservative council might perhaps have in some way possibly been a 'guide' for what Porter later did in Westminster, to consolidate their electoral support after defeating Labour in 1978. But nothing of course was ever proved and no written or other evidence was ever sought or found. Back in the 1930s the Conservatives argued that Herbert Morrison's vast London County Council estate-building programmes were aimed at winning more votes for Labour. Morrison taunted the Conservatives by claiming that he was 'building them out of London', but in truth he was giving tens of thousands of London's slum–dwellers a new home, an inside toilet and a garden – a political programme that had cross-party support and mass appeal.

What Porter planned was way beyond anything that Morrison could have imagined, and certainly without any of Morrison's moral purpose. Porter wanted to change the population in the most marginal wards in Westminster so that she would be re-elected in 1990. It was as simple and as straightforward as that.

What she did not bargain for was the Westminster Labour Group. Working with the BBC, the local and national media and Labour members of Parliament, we uncovered the plot and made it an issue that could not be ignored. We used every device at our disposal to force the authorities to take action – questions in Parliament, complaints to the ombudsman, objections to the Council's accounts to the district auditor – together with a regular stream of stories for the media. Porter and her crew must have been fed up with us – even more so when, in December 2001, Porter had exhausted all legal avenues after the House of Lords upheld the district auditor's findings of 'wilful misconduct' against her and the £42 million surcharge.

So, when the chance came for the Conservatives to get their own back on one of their tormentors, they took it with both hands. This was the background to my Standards Board ordeal.

Ironically, the charge against me of passing confidential information to third parties is contrary to the Councillors' Code of Conduct, introduced by the Labour government in 2000. The complaint to the Standards Board had been made by the Council's chief executive, Peter Rogers, following the 1 July 2003 edition of the *Today* programme, BBC Radio's flagship morning news programme. Not only did the Council refer me to the Standards Board for giving confidential information to the press, but my other 'crime' was 'to bring the Council and my office as a councillor into disrepute'.

For most people, the notion that I had somehow brought Westminster City Council into disrepute for exposing its tardiness in collecting Porter's massive debt was way beyond the bounds of fantasy. The Standards Board should have seen Westminster's party political games a mile off. But common sense and reason have no place in the board's lexicon. And once the Standards

Board investigation process had started it could not be stopped. Like a juggernaut out of control, it ploughed on relentlessly.

Under the government's Code of Conduct, defending myself by invoking the 'public interest' was specifically excluded. That is, until 8 February 2005, when, at a preliminary hearing of the Orwellian-sounding Adjudication Panel for England, Gavin Millar QC successfully persuaded the three-man panel that, in order to comply with the Human Rights Act, a 'public interest' defence was admissible.

The Standards Board was not amused. They had a 'point of principle' to defend. They promptly replaced their unsuccessful counsel from the first hearing with a new heavyweight – Antony White QC from Cherie Blair's Matrix chambers, who had earlier famously defended Naomi Campbell in her battle with the *Daily Mirror*. His junior was Heather Rogers, Andrew Gilligan's counsel at the Hutton inquiry, no doubt hired for her inside knowledge of the workings of the *Today* programme.

This led, in May 2005, to a full three-day hearing of the Adjudication Panel at the Aeonian Centre, a converted 1930s office block with a labyrinth of winding corridors and tiny ante-rooms, where I put my case and White led the prosecution. The Adjudication Panel had the power, if they found me guilty, to disqualify me from local government for up to five years. Or they could suspend me from the Council for a set period, for example twelve months. After deliberating for most of Thursday afternoon and Friday, the panel chairman, Steve Webb, announced to the packed room filled with my fellow councillors, supporters and the media that, although I had technically breached the Code of Conduct, no action should be taken against me. Not surprisingly, they also threw out the charge that I had brought the Council 'into disrepute'.

The huge cheer that went up all around me was something that I will never forget. It was as if I had scored the winning goal in the Cup Final. After two years of constant worry, sleepless nights and deeply felt anger, it was all over. My actions had been vindicated.

Throughout the near-two-year ordeal, there was nobody who believed I had done anything wrong (other than a handful of Conservative councillors and a few Council officers who were embarrassed about their failures being so publicly exposed). Without our whistleblowing in the 1980s there would have been no district auditor's investigation, no surcharge and no prospect of recovering the multi-million financial loss to Westminster residents caused by the Council's unlawful decisions and Porter's wilful misconduct.

In 1989 we brought the 'Homes for Votes' scandal to national attention by working closely with the BBC *Panorama* programme. Indeed, without John Ware's ground-breaking *Panorama* broadcast in July 1989, Porter could well have got away with it.

Our break came in March 1988, when a solitary piece of paper came into our possession identifying eight of the twenty-three wards in Westminster as 'key wards'. There had been no discussion of key wards in any Council meeting. All eight wards, however, were the most electorally marginal. They were 'key' to the Conservatives retaining control of the Council in 1990. For the next twelve months we asked question after question about the key wards, gradually building up a picture of what was taking place. The Conservatives and Council Officers, meanwhile, steadfastly maintained that there was no 'key wards' policy.

Panorama broadcast the extraordinary events in Westminster to a startled nation, sparking off the district auditor's long-running investigation. For Westminster Labour Group, working closely with the media is what effective opposition and scrutiny has always been about. So, fourteen years later, in 2003, I had no hesitation in working closely with Andy Hosken, an experienced investigative journalist with the *Today* programme.

I had been a Labour councillor for a long time. Every day of it was in opposition to the Westminster Conservatives. I was first elected to Westminster City Council in May 1982, for the Harrow Road ward, alongside Westminster's first black councillor, Diane Abbott (MP for Hackney North & Stoke Newington since 1987) and long-standing councillor Joe Glickman, a former Desert Rat and London cabbie. I spent the first five years as Labour's planning spokesman. In 1987 I was elected leader of the Labour Group, a year after Labour's best-ever 1986 election result, when we won twenty-seven of the sixty seats on the Council and came within 106 votes of winning the normally rock-solid Conservative

Cavendish ward, which would have made Labour the largest party.

That 27-strong Labour Group was packed with talent and ability. We were reckoned to be one of the best Labour opposition groups in the country. Our team included deputy leader Neale Coleman, now chief adviser and strategist to the mayor of London, Ken Livingstone. Our chief whip was Andrew Dismore, now MP for Hendon and chair of the Human Rights Select Committee. Peter Bradley, MP for The Wrekin from 1997 to 2005, was deputy whip and our finance spokesperson was David Pitt-Watson, who later went on to be the Labour Party's director of finance. Gavin Millar, the QC who represented me at the Adjudication Panel hearing, was part of our housing team.

We mixed that top-class professional expertise with the grass-roots campaigning experience of Paddington, Pimlico and Marylebone community activists Jill Selbourne, Madge Cavalla, Richard Nicholls and Jackie Rosenberg and others, such as local teachers Maggie Cahill and Isla Robertson. Our 'elder statesmen', Joe Hegarty, Hugh Garside and John Thirlwell, brought years of wisdom and town hall insight. Together, we worked as a team to uncover the 15p cemeteries scandal and blew the lid on the Council's disgraceful 'Homes for Votes' gerrymandering.

Between 1986 and 1990 we ran the Conservatives ragged. Talk of an unprecedented Labour victory in 1990 was not so fanciful. As part of the attempt to win the extra three seats needed to win control, I moved from the safe Labour Harrow Road ward to fight the ultra-marginal Conservative Cavendish ward, north of Oxford Street. Sadly, the Conservative government's financial fix, which enabled the Council to set an artificially low poll tax, blew Labour out of the water. I lost heavily, along with twelve of my Labour colleagues, including Coleman, Pitt-Watson, Cavalla and Jackie Rosenberg.

I returned to the Council in October 1997 at a by-election in the Queen's Park ward, following Karen Buck's election to Parliament for Regent's Park & Kensington North the previous May. With two young daughters, I decided to put my efforts into education issues and in 1998 I was appointed Labour's education spokesperson. Later, in 2001, following the introduction of the new cabinet/scrutiny system, I was given the job of chair of the Education Overview and Scrutiny Committee – the first Labour councillor to chair a committee at Westminster. I was enjoying the job and, believe it or not, even a few of the Conservatives said I was doing OK.

Throughout this period the 'Homes for Votes' legal actions were unfolding. In December 1997 the High Court unanimously upheld the district auditor's findings that Porter and her deputy, David Weeks, should be surcharged for over £26 million. Porter and Weeks appealed and in April 1999 the Court of Appeal decided by two to one that the district auditor was wrong. In its famous phrase, the Court of Appeal ruled that councillors were allowed to make 'voter-pleasing decisions'. The district auditor was, however, given leave to appeal and over two and a half years later, in December 2001, the House of Lords agreed with the auditor and the Court of Appeal decision was overturned.

It was now up to Westminster City Council to recover the Porter surcharge – which had now grown to over £42 million because of interest payments. Everyone knew that it was not going to be an easy task to get the money from Porter, not least because she had carefully moved her money out of the UK since before the district auditor published his provisional report in 1994. But little did we know of the agonisingly slow progress and missed opportunities that would be a feature of the Council's lacklustre recovery efforts.

As an organisation, Westminster City Council had never really come to terms with the enormity of the 'Homes for Votes' scandal. The Council was virtually a 'one-party state'. It had always been Conservative and Porter's gerrymandering meant that it would always be Conservative. The leading Conservative politicians in the early years of the new millennium – particularly the leader of the Council, Simon Milton, and his close political colleague, chief whip Robert Davis – were protégés of Shirley Porter and were both closely linked with the events of the late 1980s. One of the Council's senior officers, Colin Wilson, the current director of Legal and Administrative Services, was responsible for drafting the Council's case that, contrary to the mountains of evidence later produced for the district auditor's hearings, the Council acted lawfully throughout. Of course, the district auditor dismissed the Council's claims that it had been acting lawfully. But, even after so many years, some people at City Hall were still 'in denial' about the Porter years.

My suspicions about the Council's 'go slow' on the Porter surcharge recovery began to surface in early May 2003, when Karen Buck sent me a copy of an email she had received from a private investigator, George Liddell. Liddell was working for internet tycoon Cliff Stanford, a business associate of John Porter, Shirley Porter's son. John Porter and Stanford were locked in a boardroom battle and Stanford had employed Liddell to find information on Porter. As part of those investigations, Liddell uncovered details of the Porter family's business dealings that showed that Shirley Porter was a lot wealthier than she claimed to be (in January 2002 she swore an affidavit that she was down to her last £300,000). Liddell had offered this information to the Council and its legal advisers in January 2003 but they declined to take up his offer.

Liddell's email to Buck was sensational. According to Liddell:

> I have been investigating Mr John Porter for the past year . . . During my investigation I have by sheer necessity had to investigate matters relating to Dame Shirley Porter (DSP). In the space of that year I'm sorry to tell you that I got a lot further than WCC's lawyers investigating the matter.
>
> We told them [Stephenson Harwood, a firm of specialised forensic lawyers] that we could prove that John Porter had in the past two years carried out investment business on DSP's behalf. Did they ask to see this evidence, No! I offered to hand over my entire investigation and continue to develop the leads we had made, did they want to know, No!
>
> DSP's money is alive and well and running around London in the form of her son John Porter. We can show the money trail from him to her and we can certainly prove he acts on her behalf.

Buck had also sent Liddell's email to Jonathan Rosenberg, one of the founders of Walterton and Elgin Community Homes, a group of Paddington residents who had freed themselves from

Westminster City Council control by becoming the first to take advantage of the Tenants' Choice legislation introduced by the Conservative government in the 1980s. Rosenberg was part of the team that had worked closely with the BBC's John Ware on the July 1989 *Panorama* programme. He had also amassed a wealth of documentation on 'Homes for Votes' and other Westminster scandals and, more recently, had worked with Andy Hosken on a number of Westminster-related stories for *Today*. When Rosenberg contacted Hosken with details of the Liddell email, Hosken started his investigations. This book is my account of what happened next.

The Westminster 'Homes for Votes' story was the biggest ever scandal in local government history. My battle with the Standards Board was just one episode in the last twenty years' history of what has a claim to be the UK's rottenest borough. Some people might say that what happened in Westminster was a long time ago and we should forget about something that went on in the 1980s. But the Westminster story is unique, and it has important lessons about the use of power and the way in which those holding power can be held to account. The scale of wrongdoing was unprecedented in British local government. And, thanks to Westminster Labour Group, it will never happen again.

This is the story of the Westminster Whistleblowers, a great team of which it was my privilege to be a part. It is a great shame that our team never had the opportunity of running the Council. I like to think we would have done a good job. But this is the story of a how a group of opposition councillors defied the odds and brought town hall wrongdoing to public attention and forced the authorities to take action. It is a story of which I am very proud to be part.

Timeline

May 1983   Shirley Porter elected leader of Westminster City Council

November 1985   Westminster City Council decides to sell its three cemeteries – at Mill Hill, Hanwell and East Finchley – for 15p .

May 1986   The Conservatives lose eleven seats at the Council elections. They are reduced to thirty-two seats, with Labour on twenty-seven and one Independent.

June 1986–July 1989   Westminster City Council adopts and implements its 'Building Stable Communities' policies, aimed at winning the 1990 Council elections by moving in Conservative voters and moving out Labour voters in eight 'key wards'.

July 1989   *Panorama* exposes the Council's 'key ward' strategy. Twelve Westminster residents submit an objection to the Council's accounts to the district auditor on the grounds that the 'key ward' strategy is unlawful.

March 1990   Westminster City Council sets a poll tax of £195 after successfully lobbying the government in a campaign which stressed the electoral vulnerability of the Conservative majority at the forthcoming Council elections.

May 1990   The Conservatives sweep to victory, winning forty-five of the sixty seats on the Council. Labour lose twelve seats and the sole Independent councillor is defeated.

January 1991   Shirley Porter created a Dame of the British Empire for her services to local government. In February, Porter stands down as leader and is replaced by her deputy, David Weeks.

January 1994   The district auditor, John Magill, issues his provisional findings that 'the Council was engaged in gerrymandering which I am minded to find is a disgraceful and improper purpose'.

March 1994   Porter and her husband move to Israel and begin to move their finances out of the UK.

May 1996   The district auditor issues his final report and issues surcharge certificates to Porter and others. Porter and others appeal to the High Court.

December 1997   The High Court upholds the surcharge against Porter and Weeks for £26.4 million. Porter and Weeks appeal to the Court of Appeal.

April 1999   Porter and Weeks win in the Court of Appeal on a 2-1 majority, on the grounds that politicians were entitled to make 'voter-pleasing' decisions. The district auditor appeals to the House of Lords.

December 2001   The House of Lords unanimously overturns the Court of Appeal decision and reinstates the surcharge. Westminster City Council is now responsible for collecting the surcharge – which has now grown to almost £40 million because of interest.

December 2001–May 2003   The Council fails to collect any of the surcharge from Porter.

May 2003   Private investigator George Liddell contacts Karen Buck MP with information about Porter's finances and casting doubt on the Council's commitment to collecting the surcharge.

July 2003   BBC *Today* programme exposes the Council's lack of progress in collecting the surcharge, using some confidential information supplied by me. Westminster City Council reports me to the Standards Board for England for breaching the Code of Conduct by giving confidential information to the BBC.

April 2004   Westminster City Council accepts £12.3 million from Shirley Porter in full and final settlement for her £42 million debt.

November 2004   The Standards Board refers the Council's complaint against me to the Adjudication Panel for England.

February 2005   The Adjudication Panel agrees to allow me to mount a public-interest defence for my actions.

May 2005   The Adjudication Panel agrees that my breach of the Code of Conduct is purely technical and decides to take no action against me.

1

Shirley Porter takes control

Within weeks of winning the Tory leadership she forced all her officers to ditch their local government jargon, turned power breakfasts into a religion and worked all hours God sent as she battled to impress her mentor, the then Prime Minister Margaret Thatcher.

Evening Standard, 18 December 1997

If this is a story about Westminster City Council during the last decades of the twentieth century, then Shirley Porter must lie at its heart. For over twenty years she cast a long shadow across the Council. Even now, over a decade after she finally quit both the Council and the UK, her name is forever synonymous with the most spectacular local government scandals ever. Everyone knows her name, but few have a good word to say about her. How did she get into a position where she could do so much damage to so many people? And how was she allowed to reduce the previously unblemished reputation of Westminster City Council to that of a laughing stock? Well, here is the true story, warts and all, of her rise and fall, with all the trimmings.

It all started to go wrong for Westminster in May 1983, when Porter was elected leader of the Westminster Conservative Group. The battle was very much between the old-guard Tory patricians, led by deputy leader Jonah Walker-Smith, and the new Thatcherite Conservative right-wing led by Porter, Barry Legg and David Weeks. Porter also attracted support of the newer intake of self-made men and young Tory councillors such as Peter Hartley and Robert Davis. It is hard to believe now, but when she was first elected leader of the Council, no one really knew her. In fact, she was usually described as the 'wife of Tesco's chairman, Sir Leslie Porter'. It did not take long for that to change.

Porter was certainly not the kind of leader that Westminster City Council had ever experienced before. Born in 1930 in Clapton, east London, she was withdrawn by her father from Warren School in Worthing, West Sussex, before she could sit her exams, reportedly because the school governors turned her down for head girl on account of her Jewish name. Her father, Tesco founder Jack Cohen, sent her to finishing school in Switzerland, where it was said she 'learned to ski and little else' (*Independent*, 20 December 1997). Married at eighteen to Leslie Porter, ten years her senior, for the next twenty years she led the life of a typical well-off middle-class wife and mother, bringing up two children, John and Linda.

But the Porters' move to Westminster certainly stirred up something. Shirley Porter was first elected to Westminster City Council for the Hyde Park ward in 1974, and she lost no time in getting immersed in the nitty-gritty. As an active member of the Highways and Works Committee, which she later chaired, she drove around Westminster in her black Mini scouring the streets for potholes, cracked pavements, discarded litter and broken street lights.

Never afraid to speak her mind or attract publicity, she first came to prominence during the 'Winter of Discontent' in 1978–9, when she appeared regularly on the TV news against a background of rubbish piled high in Leicester Square. Those Leicester Square pictures were one of the most enduring images of the late 1970s and certainly helped Margaret Thatcher's Conservatives to capture the mood of the times and win the 1979 general election. And with a new Conservative government in power following the same right-wing instincts, it was not long before Porter's fortunes rose within Westminster.

Her opportunity came in May 1983, at the retirement of Council leader David Cobbold. Promising a new, business-like, go-getting and super-efficient Council, in tune with the 1980s, Porter swept to power, much to the surprise and consternation of her more staid rivals, who had expected Walker-Smith, son of Conservative grandee Sir Derek Walker-Smith MP, to take the natural next step from deputy leader to leader.

Porter saw her job as leader of Westminster City Council as

more than emptying the bins and sweeping the streets more cheaply and quickly. She saw her responsibilities on a much grander scale. She believed her job was to 'look after' the great West End landmarks and institutions – Big Ben, Oxford Street, the Royal Parks; what she regarded as 'the real London'.

Porter acted out of instinct rather than from political or management theories. She got her ideas from others, not from books. The former Westminster chief executive Rodney Brooke, who joined the City Council in 1984 with a glowing reputation as the wily chief executive of West Yorkshire County Council, tells the story of a meeting at her Hyde Park penthouse flat, where the bookcase boasted a complete set of the works of Sir Walter Scott.

> 'I see that you share my taste for Walter Scott,' I said to her in the early days of our relationship. 'Walter Scott?' she said. Clearly the name conveyed nothing to her. Disposing of the matter, she later asked me if I would like a gin and tonic. At the touch of a button, the spines of the complete works of Scott slid aside to reveal the cocktail cabinet. (Rodney Brooke, *The Councillor: Victim or Vulgarian?*, Local Government Association, 2005)

Her flat, at Chelwood House, in tree-lined Gloucester Square, was her 'breakfast office' to which harassed Council officers would be regularly summoned. The flat, likened to the lighting department in Selfridges, was described as 'indescribably vulgar' by former Conservative councillor Patricia Kirwan, with whom Porter later fell out badly. 'She had covers on the loo paper,' according to Kirwan. However, Porter's *modus operandi* dictated that very little was ever eaten: 'There was plenty available on a sort of revolving platter in the middle of the huge circular table, but those invited rarely had a chance to eat it. They spent their time instead wrestling with paperwork, trying to find the instant answers required by the leader.'

Always wanting to drive people harder and find new ways of keeping people on their toes, Brooke explained one of her less successful wheezes:

TM [time management] Filofaxes were issued to all managers. At each meeting Lady P demanded to see everyone's day plan. Compulsive recording took place. One day calm broke out. Lady P was on a plane to Israel. Newspapers were picked up. Feet were placed on desks. Then my phone rang. It was the pilot of an El Al jet bound for Tel Aviv. Lady P had commandeered communications for a particularly urgent call to her chief executive. 'Everyone', she said, 'who pulls their weight must be given a leather-bound Filofax to replace the plastic.' Other officers would then see clearly the rewards of loyalty. Sadly the call was counter-productive. Plastic TM Filofaxes became a token of defiance. Officers meeting the leader would ostentatiously put their plastic on the table. Soon all Filofaxes were banned. (*Local Government Chronicle*, 22 January 1999)

Others, however, describe a much darker side to her. Talking of Porter, a former colleague said, 'I would say there is streak of cruelty in her. She was used to having her way and woe betide anyone not in agreement.'

Another, who agreed to speak to the press only on condition of anonymity, explained:

Shirley told me that she was keeping a card index of people's details. She said she would always have something on them which could be used. It was an awful time. Life was made intolerable. There was blood all over the ceilings. If you could not get something done, then there would be trouble. Her attitude was, It's my party, right or wrong. She made my life a misery and if you challenged a policy, you were howled down by her supporters and acolytes. (*Evening Standard*, 17 January 1994)

There was one story that she reduced one very senior officer to tears. In another, when information had been leaked, she demanded her office be swept for bugs. One former Conservative councillor who spent a great deal of time working with her claimed:

Officers would be rung early in the morning, late at night and over the weekends. She would get people whizzing off in all directions on her latest whim. And then she would attack them because they had failed to push through her policies. I saw her shatter people. She used to set impossible deadlines. She wanted to test people to destruction.

Porter claimed that her way of working was all down to watching her father build up the Tesco empire and following his successful example. 'I have this habit inherited from my father. He would go into a shop and he would always find the one dented tin. Well, I'm like that. I'm exactly like that,' she said. And taking the Tesco model and applying it to Westminster City Council lock, stock and barrel was bound to create waves.

She adopted her father's mantra, 'You can't do business sitting on your arse', and demanded that her team remain on call at all hours of the day. After once telephoning a council officer at 11 p.m. only to find he was in bed she asked in astonishment: 'Why, what's the matter?' (*Times*, 20 December 1997)

The Tesco connection was bound to create problems for Porter. Tesco had two stores in Westminster at that time – in Pimlico and in Church Street, off the Edgware Road. It wasn't long before problems began to surface, as Brooke explained:

A BBC television crew followed two Westminster trading standards officers down Edgware Road. As they passed Tesco they suggested they go inside. As luck would have it the cameras showed them discovering underweight meat. A reorganisation in the trading standards department followed shortly afterwards. The chief executive took early retirement and I succeeded him. (*Local Government Chronicle*, 14 May 1999)

Porter extended her mission to clean up Westminster beyond the hapless officials at City Hall. Anyone who stood in her way was fair game:

In 1988 she gathered together Westminster's executives and the heads of the public utilities in London – the people who ran the gas, electricity, telephone and water services – and loaded them into a hired bus and drove them around the capital. When they reached dormant roadworks or uncollected rubbish, she stood up in the front of the bus and, using a microphone like a tour guide, ordered those responsible to come forward and confess. 'And whose is that tatty piece of zigzag trench-filling on the left?' she asked as the bus drove alongside the gardens of Buckingham Palace. 'Come on. Own up. Whose is it?' The man from British Telecom came forward and apologised for a poorly filled-in hole. (Jay Rayner, 'Dame Shirley of Tel Aviv', *Observer*, 28 February 1999)

She revelled in being on TV and in the newspapers. She encouraged the view that she and Margaret Thatcher – two grocers' daughters – were from the same no-nonsense, get-things-done mould, with Porter cleaning up the heart of the UK while Thatcher sorted out the rest of the country. And she would do anything to further that view of her role. Sometimes, however, her quest for publicity at all costs was not well received. One volunteer remembered:

I was working in a centre for people with severe learning disabilities in Westminster and one day Shirley turned up with some photographers and a huge cake in the shape of the Houses of Parliament. Shirley posed with everyone, seemingly offering them this fantastic cake. As soon as the photo session was over she disappeared . . . with the cake. It caused a lot of upset. We had to do an emergency dash to the local bakers. (*Daily Mirror*, 7 July 2004)

This was the backdrop to Porter's politics. She was used to getting her own way. And if she didn't, heaven help those who stood up to her. Council officers were dispensable. If she wasn't happy with the advice she was getting from her chief executive she would replace him. The same was true of less senior officers. Between 1984 and 1988, forty-eight out of seventy senior and middle management staff left the Council, including fourteen chief officers.

A former director of Property Services, George Touchard, recalled his time at City Hall, during his evidence on the sale of the cemeteries:

I've never had to work in a climate like I worked here, ever. Have you ever sat in one of our chief officers' boards and heard Lady Porter accuse me of being the most negative officer she had ever come across? If you put up any opposition, you were opposed to them politically or you were negative.

And Brooke recalled: 'At his leaving party a chief officer lay down in front of her. "Walk all over me, Shirley," he begged. "That's what you've been doing for the last eight years. Why change now?"' (*Local Government Chronicle*, 14 May 1999)

If there is any consolation to those officers whose careers were cut short, it looks as if she treated her husband in much the same domineering manner. Former Tesco boss Ian MacLaurin recalled that Leslie Porter enjoyed 'a Scotch or three' and at parties his wife would threaten 'in a voice as sotto voce as a buzzsaw . . . "Leslie, if you don't behave I'll take you home"' (*Independent*, 25 March 2005). It was little wonder that the board of Tesco declined to make her a director in 1985, despite her supporters mounting a campaign to try to force her appointment at the company's AGM. Three women shareholders complained that there were no women on the board, although the majority of Tesco customers were women. One of them suggested Porter as an 'ideal candidate'. But there was no love lost between Porter and MacLaurin, then Tesco's new chairman, and she was never appointed. In his autobiography, MacLaurin described Porter as 'obsessed with power, a sorcerer's apprentice who brewed up the concoction that eventually destroyed her' (*Mail on Sunday*, 23 May 1999).

And having failed to secure a seat on the Tesco board she was now set for a few shocks from her Labour opponents.

2

Labour nearly wins

The borough was divided into safe, marginal and target wards, which would be difficult to win but essential to gain overall control. Intensive work, including weekly distributions of leaflets and newsletters, was carried out over a twelve month period in the marginal and target wards and the two constituencies pooled their resources, with the stronger North Westminster party sending organisers and members to help the weaker southern wards.

Paula Watson, *Labour Briefing*, Autumn 1986

The only opponents Shirley Porter could not replace at her whim were her Labour antagonists. Removing elected Labour councillors at City Hall or at the GLC would require a more strategic and planned approach. At City Hall, dealings between Labour and Conservatives changed as dramatically as they did with Porter's own colleagues and Council officers. Relations between Labour and Conservative were never cosy, but there was a degree of mutual respect for each other's political beliefs. Porter had absolutely no respect for Labour councillors. And we returned the compliment. Council meetings deteriorated into pitched battles – which had the interesting effect of filling the public gallery as both political parties encouraged their members to come along and give vocal support.

For a while Council meetings were the best free show in town, complete with interventions from the Marylebone police, who were regularly called by hapless Lord Mayors to clear the public gallery. Porter and her colleagues responded to this growing public interest by requiring everyone attending Council meetings to sign a declaration promising to keep order. She even proposed installing a glass screen so that heckling from the public gallery would not be heard by delicate Conservative councillors. With a political style more akin to a street fighter than the traditional Tory 'lady bountiful', Porter gave as good as she got. She later recalled:

> I stood in the council chamber being heckled and jeered and thought of my father, working in the markets where they used to blow a whistle and people had to run to get their pitch. It was survival of the fittest. You either crumble or you stay and fight. Like him, I stayed and fought. (*Glasgow Herald*, 31 January 1994)

Ironically, the Conservative campaign to abolish the Greater London Council (GLC) created the conditions that were to cause so much political difficulty for Westminster Conservatives at the May 1986 City Council elections. Massively unpopular, the Conservatives' GLC abolition policy provoked a huge wave of support for Ken Livingstone and Labour, which went way beyond the narrow confines of Labour's natural support at the time. Huge numbers of young people gathered around the GLC banner, along with the growing 'rainbow coalition' of London's ethnic minority communities, alternative lifestyle followers and fringe political groups. Across London, all these forces came together during the 1984–6 period and Labour politics in Westminster benefited from this growing political activity. Unhappiness with the abolition of the GLC was not just confined to Labour and the usual suspects. As the former Prime Minister Edward Heath remarked in November 1984, the proposal to abolish the GLC 'immediately lays the Conservative Party open to the charge of the greatest gerrymandering in the last 150 years of British history'.

At the same time, the Labour Party in Westminster sensed that there was a once-in-a-lifetime political opportunity on the horizon. Livingstone was the GLC member for Paddington and his monthly report to the General Committee would entertain and fire up packed meetings with the latest news and gossip on the anti-abolition fight-back campaign. We looked at the forthcoming 1986 Council elections and asked ourselves: 'Why not?'

Our analysis was a lot more sophisticated than simply deciding to have a go. The Labour Group leader, Joe Hegarty, a councillor since 1974 and a Marylebone resident since birth, had observed a real change in the socio-economic make-up of the traditionally strong Conservative areas north and south of Oxford Street, in Victoria and in St James's. The residents of the big mansion blocks, traditionally the home of Conservative-voting families, were changing. Many flats were being bought by companies for their senior staff who voted elsewhere. Others were bought by foreign nationals who did not have the vote. The mansion block population was also getting older, with many elderly lone residents. Where in the 1960s and 1970s there were, say, three or more Tory votes in a mansion block flat, now there might only be one vote.

Crucially, however, the Labour vote in the council and housing association flats was still there. In addition, all the live-in caretakers and porters – and their families – were still there. We calculated that if we could maximise our vote by getting the Labour turn-out to its limit, at the same time as the Tory vote was falling, we could run the Conservatives close.

Our strategy and plan was hatched on 4 August 1984 at the home of the Westminster North Labour Party chair, Steve Hilditch, and his wife Jen McClelland, the Labour Party secretary. At that meeting Hilditch and McClelland, together with Hegarty, Neale Coleman and me, worked out the broad scope of the plan. We agreed that we would need to concentrate our efforts on a small number of wards where the Conservatives were vulnerable because of changing socio-economic trends and inactive sitting Conservative councillors, and where keen local Labour Party members could be encouraged to put themselves forward as candidates.

Our electoral arithmetic calculated that in a very good year for Labour we could reckon to win twenty-seven out of the sixty seats on the Council. That, in itself, would be a magnificent result, given that we had just sixteen seats at the time. However, getting the extra four seats to secure a majority was a massive mountain to climb. Because of the size of the Conservative majorities in the rest of the wards, there were no more marginals left.

So we looked hard to see if we could turn any of the safe Conservative wards into marginals. We identified a number of possible targets, including the three-member Cavendish ward north of Oxford Street, which took in the bohemian Fitzrovia area; the two-member Victoria ward south of Victoria Street, which included a number of large Peabody Estates; and the two-member St James's ward, including the fiercely independent Covent Garden area. If we could win all three wards we would gain seven extra seats and win control. Winning the Cavendish ward alone would give us thirty seats and make Labour the largest party, if the lone Independent councillor, Lois Peltz, held her seat in the West End ward, which she and Brigadier Gordon Viner won in 1978, when faction-fighting in the local Conservative Association split the vote and allowed the Independents to triumph.

Our strategy would involve the Labour Party in Westminster spending the next two years, from 1984 to 1986, building up effective local campaigns in each of the three wards. Our plan was to deliver regular newsletters, lead local campaigns, organise petitions, take up individual casework, join the local groups and organisations, undertake electoral registration drives to get Labour supporters on the electoral register and get local press coverage for our campaigning efforts. We reckoned that two years would give us the time to get a local organisation going so that, come election day, we would know who our supporters were and be able to get them out to vote because of all the work we had put in on their behalf.

A key part of the strategy would be to select candidates early so that committed individuals would take responsibility for each local campaign. We also arranged for the three target wards to select first so that they had the pick of the best candidates. In this way, the Cavendish ward selected three first-rate candidates for the 1986 Council elections – Karen Buck, now Member of Parliament for Regent's Park & Kensington North and a former minister in the Department for Transport; Jenny Edwards, who was Labour's parliamentary candidate for Westminster North in 1987 and 1992; and Ron Harley, who is now a senior officer with Unison. In the Victoria and St James's wards we had a similar success in attracting top-rate candidates, including Linda Hardman in Victoria and Ruth Bush (now a Councillor in the Harrow Road ward) in St James's.

We knew we had a real chance when two of the rising young Conservative councillors, Robert Davis and Simon Mabey, deserted their marginal Bayswater and Little Venice wards for the safe Lancaster Gate and Knightsbridge wards. And we almost succeeded. On 8 May 1986 the Conservative majority was reduced from twenty-seven seats to just four. Labour won the Little Venice, Bayswater, Millbank and Churchill wards from the Conservatives to increase the number of Labour councillors from sixteen to twenty-seven. The one Independent councillor for the West End ward, Peltz, held her seat.

Despite a 20 per cent swing, Labour failed to win the formerly rock-solid Cavendish ward from the Conservatives, but by just 106 votes. If we had won Cavendish we would have been the largest party on the Council with thirty out of the sixty seats. Labour also came a lot closer than ever before in St James's and Victoria, and the SDP–Liberals achieved their best-ever result in the Hamilton Terrace ward in St John's Wood.

The result we achieved surprised everyone outside West-minster, who had no idea we could even get to twenty-seven seats. We were now the second largest Labour opposition group in London with some very talented new councillors and we were poised to make an even bigger impact on the Council. We were going into the next four years with confidence and real expectations of making a difference for the people we had just been elected to represent.

And what about the Conservatives? Until 1998, Westminster City Council used to indulge in a leisurely Friday morning count of the votes at Porchester Hall, Paddington, starting at 9.00 a.m. Why should they rush to count the votes on Thursday evening like everyone else? There was never going to be political change in Westminster. As ever, the Conservatives went to bed and slept soundly on Thursday 9 May. But by ten o'clock on Friday morning, after hearing the first results and seeing the size of the swing to Labour, the Conservatives were in a state of shock.

There was panic all around as defeated Conservative councillors and candidates looked for an explanation. At times of defeat, all eyes turn to the leader, and all eyes were on Shirley Porter that Friday morning. Never one to find fault with herself, Porter looked for other scapegoats, most particularly the Council's chief officers, whom she blamed for not implementing her policies quickly or effectively enough. As Rodney Brooke explained: 'As Tory ward after ward fell, Dame Shirley crossed the room to where I sat as returning officer. "If we lose today," she said, "it's your fault."' Such electoral and political humiliation would never be allowed to happen again.

The next four years would certainly be interesting.

3

Porter hatches the 'Homes for Votes' plot

Fear of defeat proved [the] inspiration [for 'Homes for Votes']. In the elections of May 1986, Westminster council's Conservative majority dropped from twenty-six seats to four. Lady Porter was distraught. Within weeks she was laying down plans to ensure that Labour would never again come so close to winning the prize. And so: Building Stable Communities.

Jay Rayner, 'Dame Shirley of Tel Aviv', *Observer*, 28th February 1999

Shirley Porter quickly started to plot her revenge on Labour for the very public humiliation she suffered on the morning of 9 May 1986. Within days she had organised a breakfast meeting with Conservative Wandsworth councillors, who had won control of Wandsworth in 1978 and had successfully held on to the council in 1982 and 1986. One of the Wandsworth Conservatives' flagship policies was the sale of council houses and flats (part of overall Conservative policy under Margaret Thatcher). Once sold, council flats, which traditionally were occupied by Labour-voting council tenants, had tended to be occupied by their owners, who were more likely to vote Conservative, and this may well have helped Wandsworth to win two Council elections. Whether by design or chance, it had been successful for the Conservatives.

Indeed, as Patricia Kirwan, a former Conservative Housing chairman in Westminster, later told the BBC's *Panorama*, the meeting with Wandsworth Conservatives was 'definitely 100 per cent the beginning of the designated thing – to target marginal wards and the sort of tactics that one had to use to go about it'.

There were rumours that Wandsworth was implementing a policy that was later to be pioneered by Porter, but there was never any documentary evidence to support these allegations.

Although the Conservatives had lost eleven councillors, the right wing of the Westminster Conservative Group had been strengthened by the election of three clever and resourceful councillors – lawyer Alex Segal, Dr Michael Dutt and advertising executive Miles Young. All three made a rapid rise through the Conservative ranks and played an important role in the development of the Council's post-1986 policies, particularly housing.

A taste of what the Conservative housing plans might look like had surfaced in late 1985. On 6 September the Conservatives called a special meeting of the Housing Committee, at the Seymour Hall in Marylebone. The only item on the agenda was Kirwan's proposal to sell off the Walterton and Elgin estates in north Paddington to property developers in order 'to create a new community'. In her days as GLC member for Paddington, from 1977 to 1981, Kirwan was behind plans to sell GLC-owned land on Elgin Avenue and Walterton Road for housing for sale. The Walterton and Elgin proposals were simply more of the same and a taste of things to come.

However, this time she bit off more than she could chew. As soon as the Housing Committee report was made public and the full horror of Kirwan's 'new community' proposals were laid bare, we distributed a letter to local residents encouraging them to attend the forthcoming Housing Committee. More than 200 residents made the journey down the Harrow Road to the Seymour Hall to voice their angry protest. Their next step was to form the Walterton and Elgin Action Group (WEAG).

A month later, in October 1985, having approved the sell-off plan in principle, the Housing Committee met again to discuss the proposed estate sale. This was an even more lively event than the September meeting, with the public gallery at City Hall full to capacity and GLC member Ken Livingstone (Kirwan's successor at Paddington) present. As a councillor for the Harrow Road ward, in which the two estates were situated, I spoke against the plans. With strong vocal support from the emotionally charged public gallery, it was difficult for Kirwan to stem the tide of opposition. She lost control completely. The police were called and I was escorted out of the meeting. At this point Livingstone suggested that everyone else (other than the Conservative councillors and Council officers) should leave the meeting, too, and reconvene down the road at County Hall.

Following the 1986 elections, the Council's Chief Officer's Board met for the first time on 15 May. They were given the startling news that Porter believed that the close election result was the fault of the chief executive, Rodney Brooke, and his fellow chief officers. Ominously, they were also told that there was to be a 'change of direction'. This was followed by a meeting of the Chairmen's Group (Porter and her leading councillors) to discuss the marginal wards. Following this meeting Kirwan wrote a note to her colleagues which warned that 'the dangers of mass voting one way or another (i.e. nurses about to be evicted from health service accommodation . . . and homeless/down-and-outs who are not our natural supporters) cannot be overemphasised'.

Having worked out their strategy, Porter, together with the deputy leader, David Weeks, and chief whip Barry Legg, attended the Chief Officers' Board meeting on 24 June 1986 to lay down the line. At that meeting they told the Council's chief officers that winning the next Council elections in 1990 was the top priority and that this would be the focus of the Council's attentions for the next four years. Porter and company told the chief officers that their objectives included 'social engineering including housing'.

Work on the Conservative social engineering plan got under-way speedily. Porter and colleagues organised a working lunch less than a week later, on 30 June, to discuss a prospective planning study which would provide the justification for a highly targeted political campaign. The meeting was attended by Graham England, the director of Housing, who noted down at the time 'economic justification for Gmander on Hsg', 'who is a Tory voter?', 'Gentrification' and 'will company lets vote Tory?'. England's habit of keeping a written record of these meetings was later to prove invaluable to the district auditor.

A few days later the Council secured the services of a senior civil servant to manage its new housing policies. On 3 July Bill Phillips joined the City Council on a two-year secondment from the Department of the Environment, as head of the Policy Unit. Phillips got to work straightaway and later that month, on 29 July, he met Porter to discuss properties in key wards, voting records and decanting. So, just two months after suffering their worst-ever electoral setback, Porter's Westminster Conservatives had worked out their plan of action and persuaded Thatcher to lend them one of her senior officials to oversee and manage its implementation.

After the summer break, the Conservatives organised a party seminar on 6 September to discuss a paper written by the Council's Planning Department, entitled 'A Strategy for 1990 – the Wandsworth Experience'. The paper made the Council's task crystal clear and warned that 'there is an immediate need to socially engineer the population in marginal wards'. Kirwan also presented a paper to the seminar entitled 'Westminster Housing 1986–90', which set out the plan 'to ensure that as far as possible, Westminster's housing policies achieve the type of social and economic residential mix that will enable us to retain control of the Council in 1990 and help to retain the Conservative majority in the Parliamentary seat of North Westminster'. The Conservative plan could not have been clearer.

Later that month, the Chairmen's Group instructed the director of Housing to be 'mean and nasty' to the homeless. In addition, the group gave other instructions to officers, such as to find 'suitable wards for housing the homeless long term, Westminster Council families in Labour wards'. They were told to take a 'very hard line on homelessness, try to ship them out', and to determine how to 'get the homeless out of Westminster', as well as offering 'cash to homeless person to get lost'. Significantly, the Chairmen's Group also discussed a policy of 'permanent rehousing of homeless outside Westminster'.

September 1986 was a busy month as the policy started to move into gear. The consultants PA Cambridge had been hired to provide the economic and social back-up for the new policies. At a meeting that month there was a discussion about how 'to push Labour voters out of marginal wards. Housing Dept can't say privatise/gentrify Council blocks in marginal wards – 400 in B & B but we could say – preserve economic base – need to boot out these blocks.' The meeting also talked about the need 'to preserve local communities – but boot out certain categories'. The Conservatives also expressed concern about community groups that 'don't vote Tory', and Porter told the consultants: 'We want the right answers.'

By November 1986, the strategy and plan was being cascaded down to second- and third-tier Council officers. On 25 November, at a meeting arranged for the Council's 'top 70' officers at the London City YMCA, the officers were told that Phillips was to be appointed to the new post of managing director of the Council. But the main message of the meeting came from Kirwan, who announced, to a no doubt stunned gathering, that the Council was going to adopt a policy of selling council property in marginal wards in order to boost the Conservative vote.

Not content with securing Phillips from the Department of the Environment, on 19 December Porter made a further plea to the government for more help to further her gerrymandering agenda. She wrote to Thatcher, arguing:

> We in Westminster are trying to gentrify the City. We must protect our electoral position which is being eroded by the number of homeless that we have been forced to house . . . Both I and my Chairman of Housing have constantly lobbied successive Secretaries of State with very little result. I feel that the problem is now so serious that you should look at it yourself. Could I suggest that one of your Policy Advisors spends some time with my officers looking at the problem in detail? I am afraid that unless something can be done, it will be very difficult for us to keep Westminster Conservative!

In January 1987, the fast-rising Alex Segal, whom Porter had quickly promoted to vice-chairman of the Housing Committee, wrote a paper on home ownership. The paper identified the Council's short-term objective as being 'to target the marginal wards and, as a matter of the utmost urgency, redress the imbalance by encouraging a pattern of tenure which is more likely to translate into Conservative votes'. It called for the Council to 'identify far more blocks particularly in key marginal wards'. Never one to hold back, Segal's report argued that 'the problem can be simply stated. If it is accepted that owner-occupiers are more inclined to vote Conservative, then we approach the 1990 election with an enormous handicap.'

On 7 January 1987, the Council formally announced its intention to appoint a managing director. Beleaguered chief executive Rodney Brooke, who had lost the confidence of Porter and her close colleagues, explained that he would be concentrating on setting up 'a multi-programme inspectorate, incorporating the present twenty-nine separate inspectors' departments, responsible for everything from sex licences to cracks in pavements'. He added cheekily: 'In the past, if you ran a late-night topless café in Soho, you could have been visited by twenty different inspectors.' And it was no surprise when, on 1 February, Phillips was appointed managing director on a four-year contract.

Two weeks later, on 14 and 15 February 1987, the Conservative Group held a conference at the University Arms Hotel in Cambridge. At that meeting the eight 'key wards' were identified for the first time and the increased number of target Conservative voters was announced. They were Cavendish, Victoria, St James's, Millbank, West End, Bayswater, Little Venice and Hamilton Terrace. An overall target of 2,200 new Conservative voters in the eight key wards was identified.

Officers were informed about the key wards and the target figures but implementation issues were proving difficult to sort out. On 17 March 1987, a strictly confidential report, written by Graham England, entitled 'Designation of Council Properties in Key Wards', informed Conservative councillors that 'in an initial summary to members on 26 February 1987, officers identified which properties they could support for designation in the eight key wards'. The conclusion of the report was that 'as previously stated, it is not possible in professional terms to justify the designation of all properties in the eight wards. The key ward analysis will have to flow from the PA Cambridge study.'

Despite the fact that the details had yet to be worked out and senior Council Officers were beginning to express concerns, the Conservative Group agreed the Council's 'Building Stable Communities' (BSC) policies, including the targeting of marginal wards, at a party seminar at the London Business School on 21

March. In essence the Council's policy was to sell 100 per cent of the properties it owned in the eight key wards. Significantly, Kirwan spoke against the policy for the first time.

Officer warnings about the legality of the policy were also beginning to surface. On 24 March, in response to questions from leading members about whether the 100 per cent sales target was legal, the Council's city solicitor, Matthew Ives, told Stuart Greenman, Porter's political assistant: 'It is fundamental that the arguments in favour of selling be soundly based and properly argued. Anything that smacks of political machinations will be viewed with great suspicion by the courts.'

The legal issues were raised with Jeremy Sullivan QC on 5 May 1987 and he advised that the Council could not (as had been planned) lawfully sell 250 properties a year in the marginal wards alone. Robert Lewis, the deputy city solicitor, told Sullivan that he believed that the Conservatives on the Council wanted to secure electoral advantage by a policy of designated sales in marginal wards and that Sullivan confirmed Lewis's view that it would be unlawful to concentrate sales in marginal wards. Lewis did not take a full note of the consultation with Sullivan and decided not to put in writing Sullivan's advice that what the Conservatives proposed to do would be unlawful.

So, based on the legal advice, the Chairmen's Group decided that a larger target of 500 sales a year across Westminster should be adopted in order to produce the number of sales desired in the marginal wards. Kirwan's opposition to Porter's policy, which first surfaced earlier in the year, now came to a head at the Conservative Group's annual meeting. Kirwan mounted a leadership challenge, supported by the leaders of the old guard, Tony Prendergast and Roger Bramble. But Porter triumphed and was re-elected. Kirwan was then replaced as chairman of the Housing Committee by Councillor Peter Hartley.

By the end of May, two further strands of the gerrymandering plan were beginning to take shape. On the 29th, discussions began on the proposal to set up the Westminster Housing Trust. According to Nick Reiter, the new head of the Council's Policy Unit (who, like Bill Phillips, had been seconded to Westminster from the Department of the Environment), the Westminster

Housing Trust was a device 'to sanitise what might be otherwise politically motivated'. For the Conservatives, the beauty of setting up an independent housing trust was that it would be able to discriminate in a way that the Council could not, when deciding who qualified to buy a Council property. The target for the trust was 1,300 votes in the eight marginal wards. The Conservatives planned to use £4 million of public money to subsidise the trust.

By now, the gerrymandering plans were proceeding at a pace. At a Conservative Party seminar held in Oxford on the weekend of 13 and 14 June, two key papers were presented to Conservative councillors. In the first paper, entitled 'Setting the Scene', Porter presented her group with the Conservative plan:

> We face a tremendous challenge. The electoral register for the 1990 elections will be compiled in just over two years' time. Some very ambitious policies must be implemented by then: providing a great deal of affordable housing in key areas; protecting the electoral base in other areas (for example, by controlling the impact of homelessness). There is very little time to achieve these radical policy objectives.
>
> What is gentrification? In short it is ensuring that the right people live in the right areas. The areas are relatively easy to define: target wards identified on the basis of electoral trends and results.

Mindful of the significance of what she had written, Porter told her colleagues: 'When you've read the documents and after we've had our discussion, it would be helpful if you swallow them in good spy fashion otherwise they might self-destruct!!' And to reinforce the importance of the document, Porter wrote a hand-written note on the paper: 'These papers are written assuming that ALL know ALL.'

The second report to the seminar was entitled 'Tinted Persons in the Woodpile' and referred to the number of foreign residents who would be likely to vote Labour, particularly those living in bed and breakfast accommodation.

A few weeks later, on 6 July 1987, Conservative councillors turned their attention to monitoring their gerrymandering efforts. Porter, Hartley and David Weeks met Phillips to discuss how to monitor the impact of BSC policies on each key ward in terms of how this would add to the number of potential Conservative voters. Two days later, on 8 July, against a barrage of Labour opposition led by our housing spokesman, Neale Coleman, the Housing Committee agreed to extend the Council's existing limited designated sales programme by designating for sale a further 9,360 properties, which was expected to produce approximately 500 sales per annum.

In addition, the Housing Committee introduced a scheme for capital grants of £15,000 to encourage tenants to move. Later that month, on 29 July, Porter wrote to all Conservative Councillors, in order to reassure some of the more nervous, telling them that the designated sales policy was 'judge proof'. To add weight to her reassurance, she attached a copy of Lewis's note of his 5 May consultation with Sullivan. That note, of course, did not refer to Sullivan's advice about the unlawfulness of targeting sales in electorally marginal wards.

Meanwhile, detailed analysis of how the gerrymandering policies would operate was being worked on by Council officers. For example, on 3 August 1997, Reiter wrote a report on the key ward strategy in which he advised that 'the overwhelming message from these figures is that the Council will have to rely very heavily on the housing trust/private sector and planning gain routes to achieve the electoral objectives in the key wards'. That paper was circulated widely amongst officers, including Ives, who wrote in the margins of the paper, 'This paper should not have been written by an officer. Much more subtle approach required. This paper shows officers working for a Tory victory. I am troubled by the appearance of this paper.' Sadly, Ives was not troubled enough to do anything to stop officers working for a Tory victory. Perhaps if he and his colleagues had done something, events would have unfolded differently.

So, the gerrymandering plot thickened. On 1 September 1987, the Chairmen's Group agreed to instruct officers to look at the implications of emptying Bruce House, a hostel in Covent Garden with more than 100 single men, all eligible to vote in the St James's ward, as quickly as possible and disposing of the property through the housing trust for conversion into luxury flats. Significantly, Porter and her colleagues instructed Council officers to 'make sure that the "right people" in the "right" housing associations were identified'.

By now the local political temperature was reaching boiling point and the stage was set for a landmark confrontation between the Conservatives, local residents and Labour, culminating in the Conservatives again calling for the police to clear the public gallery and the arrest of half a dozen Labour councillors. The occasion was the Housing Committee meeting on 2 September 1987, and the public gallery was packed with Walterton and Elgin residents. In his book, *Rent Boy*, former Elgin Estate resident Pete May describes the scene that night and on subsequent occasions over the following months:

> At one point, the chair of housing gave the protesters one minute to put their case . . . It all turned into something like a scene from a Tom Sharpe novel when the chair of housing left the 17th floor of City Hall and tried to reconvene the meeting on the 14th floor, without several of the Labour councillors. Those in the public gallery followed, along with several TV crews and radio reporters, pushing their way into a tiny, overcrowded committee room. A few old ladies started singing 'We Shall Not Be Moved'.
>
> At a special meeting of the policy and resources committee, called to discuss the 'disorder' at the previous housing committee meeting, Lady Porter announced that the 60 WEAG members in the audience must 'listen in silence'. A Conservative councillor then called the protesters a 'ragbag of extremists', causing uproar in the gallery.
>
> The police were called again. 'I fought six years in the war for this – a police state!' shouted one irate 83-year-old pensioner called William Rae, standing on a chair. Lady Porter claimed that a councillor had been threatened. Mr Rae identified himself as the alleged assailant. After some deliberation, the Conservative Councillor explained that his remark was directed at the Labour Group, not the residents. (Pete May, *Rent Boy: How One Man Spent 20 Years Falling off the Property Ladder*, Mainstream, 2004)

Up until November 1987, Westminster Conservatives presented a united public stance in the face of massive local opposition and growing bad publicity within London. However, in mid-

November, the splits within the Conservative ranks began to surface publicly. Porter's critics came from all directions. The old guard criticised her style, while some of the new right-wingers felt she had not made enough progress in privatising Council services. All were unhappy about the acres of negative publicity being generated by the cemeteries fiasco (see Chapter 4).

Porter never took the attack from the old guard very seriously – she didn't believe they had the courage to really stick the knife in – but her opponents now included Patricia Kirwan, who was openly gunning for revenge. In addition, the patrician Tony Prendergast indicated that he would be willing to take her place should the Conservatives want a safe pair of hands to lead them in their battle with Labour.

Despite the open challenge to her leadership, Porter and her acolytes continued to extend their tentacles into other areas of Council activity. One such area was enforcement. At a strategy day for chairmen and vice-chairmen, held at City Hall on 5 December 1987, Councillor Robert Davis, vice-chairman of the Environment Committee, presented a report, 'Review of the Environmental Protection Group'. Davis's political analysis was straight to the point. He told his colleagues:

> The Professional Advisers are presently spending a majority of their limited time and resources on two specific issues – (1) short-term lets in Park West and (2) housing of the homeless in Abbey Road, St John's Wood. However, whereas these are issues deep at the heart of the BSC strategy, they are in areas which are far from being targeted wards. Park West is in Hyde Park ward and Abbey Road in Lord's ward, two of the safest Conservative seats in Westminster. Surely, the limited resources of the Professional Advisers in the EPG should be concentrated on enforcing the planning laws in line with BSC strategy in our target wards ensuring that the right type of homes are provided bringing with it the right sort of voters. Whilst I appreciate the need to bring the test cases in Park West, I wonder whether the successful outcome (if at all) will enable us to use any newly increased powers in sufficient time to have any effect in building stable communities in our key wards by 1990.

As the Conservatives entered 1988 they continued to put more elaborate gerrymandering arrangements into place. On 12 January a meeting was held at which David Weeks, Bill Phillips and consultant Victor Hausner agreed that the monitoring system to drive BSC should be steered at member level by Weeks and Peter Hartley. In addition, a number of senior officers were designated to oversee the gerrymandering effort, meeting as often as once a week during 1988. It was not until May 1989 that the officers' steering group stopped having regular meetings, because by then the gerrymandering campaign was regarded as self-running.

In February 1988, the Conservatives extended their gerry-mandering policies beyond the Council and started to whip the housing associations into line. At a secret meeting at City Hall on 18 February, Hartley explained how the Council expected local housing associations to play their part in bringing in Conservative voters. Tony Bird, for eleven years the central London manager of the Family Housing Association, was there that evening. He later explained:

> They made it very clear they wanted associations which had mainly done rented accommodation to concentrate on owner occupation tenures, and to think creatively about rehousing Westminster households outside the borough, for which they would receive borough support. It was a difficult meeting for many people because it was quite a shock. I would say that it was bordering on intimidation of housing associations . . . the crudity of the language and the implied threat of withdrawn support unless they cooperated.

Next, the Conservatives started to organise politically in the eight target wards. To do this they would need money and lots of it. In March 1988, Porter commissioned a report, 'Keeping West-minster Conservative', which was unashamed in declaring that the Council's housing policy was the encouragement of 'a pattern of tenure likely to lead to Conservative votes'.

The report's opening paragraph pulled no punches and painted the nightmare scenario for the Conservatives in banner headlines: 'Imagine socialists running Buckingham Palace, militants lording it over Parliament and controlling Downing Street, left-wing extremists interfering with the daily running of business; a horrible nightmare. It certainly is but it could happen to the City of Westminster.' Describing the Labour attack, the report continued:

> The Westminster Labour group is clever, insidious and expert at cynical manipulation of local issues, it is packed with left-wing extremists. Several of its councillors and activists belong to Westminster Labour Left Campaign Briefing, a militant, Trotskyist organisation which believes in violent revolution, the overthrow of democratic capitalism and its replacement by a one party worker state. They are expert at manipulating the press and presenting an apparently respectable face to gain public sympathy. They cannot be under-estimated.
>
> There is only one solution to winning the local elections in 1990 and that is for a programme of political grassroots action to begin in the eight key battlezone wards as soon as possible. This can only be achieved by employing five paid political activists to work in the eight key wards.

Amongst the duties of the five 'political officers' were:

> To cultivate good relations with residents associations both in public sector and private blocks of flats in each key ward. If necessary, infiltrate those which are hostile to Conservative initiatives, to find out about the background of Labour councillors, candidates and activists for skeletons in the cupboard which can be publicly exposed.

In all, the Conservative plan was costed at £140,000 over two years.

So, despite huge opposition from local residents and from Labour, and despite doubts amongst some of her own colleagues (including a leadership challenge) and hostile media coverage about her style and approach, by March 1988 Porter and her colleagues had put in place a gerrymandering web that included almost every facet of the Council's activity and all aimed at winning the 1990 City Council elections.

So what happened next? Before moving forward we need to look at how the notorious 15p cemeteries sale took place.

4

Selling the 15p cemeteries

> To put it simply, Westminster City Council gave away three
> cemeteries, three lodge-houses, one flat, one crematorium and over
> 12 acres of prime development land in London in return for the
> princely sum of £1.
>
>   Dale Campbell-Savours MP, a Westminster resident,
>   speaking in the House of Commons on 28 May 1988

I have to admit that when, in September 1987, I was first
contacted by relatives of people buried in Westminster's three
cemeteries I had no idea that the City Council had three
cemeteries, let alone where any of them were. In the five years
that I had been a councillor I could not recall any casework
relating to the Council's cemeteries – probably because all three
were maintained to a very high standard and so there was no
reason for anyone to complain to a councillor about them.

Yet within weeks of receiving a letter and photograph album
from Eileen Sheppard, whose husband was buried at Mill Hill
cemetery, showing the extent of the neglect of the cemetery
under its new ownership, cemeteries became the all-consuming
issue at Westminster. Everything was illustrated perfectly by Mrs
Sheppard's photograph album, which contained a series of
before-and-after photographs, showing the transformation of the
cemetery from beautifully manicured lawns and neatly trimmed
borders to an overgrown wilderness that looked more like a forest
than a graveyard.

How did all this happen? It all started back on 13 September
1984, when, as part of a cost-cutting exercise to save the annual

£425,000 maintenance costs, the Council's Environment Committee agreed to investigate the possibility of selling some or all of the four cemeteries owned by the City Council (East Finchley, Hanwell, Mill Hill and Willesden Lane). The Willesden Lane cemetery was transferred to Brent Council soon after. Possibly because the Council officers responsible had serious concerns about the other three cemeteries, a report on the investigations did not surface until November 1985, when a draft report was prepared for Peter Hartley, chairman of the Environment Committee.

The draft report was accompanied by a covering letter with additional explanatory information. The letter contained advice that must have been very unwelcome to Hartley. It warned:

> In view of the current loss-making nature of the cemeteries it is unlikely that any of the prospective purchasers would be able to continue the future upkeep of the cemeteries to the standard currently achieved by the Director of Leisure. If a break-even situation is to be approached maintenance levels must therefore be expected to decline.

Significantly, there was no reference to this stark warning in the final report considered by councillors. But the sale was agreed and on 28 April 1986, just days before the City Council elections, contracts were exchanged for the sale of the three Council cemeteries at East Finchley, Mill Hill and Hanwell to Lewis & Tucker, a firm of West End estate agents. Completion of the sale did not take place until 29 January 1987. Within 24 hours Lewis & Tucker had made a profit of £170,000 by selling one of the cemetery gatehouses.

Within weeks of the sale being completed, Council officers' worst fears were coming true. In mid-February 1987 Bob Bradfield, the Council's assistant director of Leisure, wrote to Hartley:

> By the time you receive this memo, one month will have passed since the completion date for the sale of the Council's cemeteries. In the first two weeks some minimal service operated, with at least four burials taking place under the rather dubious control of a Mr White,

who had a two-week job with Cemetery Assets UK Limited to keep the service ticking over.

Since that time – and indeed before completion, rumour has been rife about the financial viability of the new owners and I am now advised that a Mr Wybrow has bought up Cemetery Assets Limited. Unfortunately, since the departure of Mr White it has not been possible to reach anyone on the telephone at Hanwell Cemetery. Letters to Cemetery Assets UK Limited are not being answered and as far as the public is concerned the cemeteries have been abandoned.

Gates at Mill Hill are reported from two sources to be left open all night and clearly vandalism of graves, fly-tipping and vandalism of toilets, shelters and staff accommodation are all possible and the press implications of this in Mrs Thatcher's constituency are considerable.

Over the next few months the situation got no better. In fact, it got even worse, with questions beginning to be raised by Conservative councillors as to why the cemeteries were experiencing such difficulties. On 29 June 1987 David Boniface, acting director of Property Services, wrote to Shirley Porter to tell her:

If the Council had decided that it wished to have future control of the cemeteries greater care could have been taken in checking out the financial stability and intentions of the original purchaser. The conveyance could have included a clause to the effect that any subsequent sale could only be carried out with the agreement and/or knowledge of the City Council.

Bradfield continued to tell Porter the unpalatable truth:

The transfers should have contained detailed provisions for the opening and closing of each cemetery; the cutting of grass at regular intervals; tree maintenance; and to perform and observe all the Council's obligations in relation to Council rights under the maintenance agreements.

With the summer well underway, the grass, along with everything else, continued to grow. Officers within the Council began to discuss matters among themselves with developing concern. A memo of 19 August 1987 from Bradfield to Boniface summarised the seriousness of the problem. He explained:

> Whilst it would be difficult to say that the cemeteries are derelict, clearly tree seedlings, brambles, bracken and other undergrowth are establishing at a rapid rate and unless more regular grass maintenance activities (including the use of grass growth retardants) are undertaken, a general air of abandonment and dereliction will set in, which in the public's eyes is far from satisfactory.

It was then, in September 1987, that I received the letter and photograph album from Eileen Sheppard. As leader of the opposition, I had the right to attend any committee of the Council and to involve myself in Environment Committee matters. I could not understand how the situation had got so bad so quickly. I wanted to find out what had been going on. I asked to see all the Council's files relating to the cemetery sale. The Council, a little surprisingly, duly obliged. It may be that some of its officers had wanted us to uncover the cemeteries scandal and so they raised no objection to my request. Neale Coleman and I then spent hours trawling through the files to uncover the details of the sale. Over the next few months, together with David Pitt-Watson and Gavin Millar, we pieced together the complicated jigsaw of what had happened.

The files included draft reports, memos between officers and advice to councillors. They also included angry letters from relatives whose loved ones were buried at the three cemeteries. Such a letter was one of 21 May 1986 to the manager of the Mill Hill cemetery from Nigella Lawson, who was at that time assistant literary editor of the *Sunday Times*. Writing on *Sunday Times* headed notepaper, she explained:

> Two weeks ago I visited my mother's grave in order to plant some flowers on it. It was her last request before she died last August. While I was planting the seeds a certain gentleman approached me and told me I was wasting my time because the grave was going to be turfed over and mowed. I found his behaviour upsetting. I had bought the

plot and I feel I should be able to do what I want on it. I can understand that untended graves need to be kept tidy but since I will be looking after my mother's grave I think it most unreasonable that you should insist on turfing it over.

The Council's files unearthed a wealth of information, all of it hidden from Labour councillors until now. Coleman produced a chronology of events so that we could track down the sequence of events blow by blow and Pitt-Watson began to delve into the machinations which enabled those involved to make a financial killing.

Meanwhile, my job was to raise the scandal in the press. Fortunately, I hit the jackpot relatively quickly. Having sent a press release to the *Evening Standard*, I was contacted by one of the paper's top investigative journalists, Stewart Payne. He liked the story and wanted to run with it. On 10 November I arranged to meet Payne in my office on the 17th floor at City Hall to show him our files and Mrs Sheppard's photograph album.

The story was complicated and during the meeting I needed to check a few facts. I called Peter Chester, one of the Council's valuers. I asked him a few questions and then Payne whispered to me: 'Ask him how much the Council sold them for.' I slipped the question into the conversation and out came the answer, '15p'. I repeated the figure aloud so that Stewart could hear and also to check that I heard correctly first time. 'Yes, that's right, we sold the cemeteries for 15p,' was Chester's calm response.

I could see that Payne had his story and his headline. I could not believe it and I doubted if others would, too. The story in the *Standard* was front-page news. Others in the London TV and radio media followed, along with the press. Mrs Sheppard and Jo Mahoney, my main contacts with the cemetery relatives, were delighted with the media coverage and were fired up for action. They wanted those responsible to pay for the hurt they had caused.

Armed with the information we had gleaned from the Council files, Mrs Sheppard, Ms Mahoney and another cemetery relative, Linda Taylor, reported the sale to the local government ombudsman. We called a special meeting of the Council on 16 December

1987, at which Councillor Miles Young, an Environment Committee member, unashamedly said to the Council: 'How can it be right to expend a half a million pounds in ratepayers' money on maintenance of three cemeteries well outside the City boundaries? It cannot be right. The cemeteries reflect a very fair standard of maintenance.'

Such insensitive comments only served to raise the emotions of the cemetery relatives, many of whom were life-long Conservative voters. They could not understand why a Conservative council was acting so heartlessly. In January 1988, under continued pressure from relatives, the media and Labour, the Council agreed to hold an internal inquiry under the direction of Bill Taylor, a former Kent County Council chief executive.

Meanwhile, we arranged a public meeting at Porchester Hall, Paddington for 21 January 1988. We wrote to as many relatives as we could and invited speakers from Ealing Council (where the Hanwell cemetery was located) and from Barnet Council (for Mill Hill and East Finchley). A local Methodist minister, Norman Grigg, agreed to chair the meeting. Word of mouth spread quickly and approximately a thousand people packed into the hall to share their anger and listen to what happened and how. Not just content to listen, the meeting agreed to set up the Westminster Association of Relatives, with Mrs Sheppard, Ms Mahoney and Ms Taylor taking leading roles alongside retired businessman Lew Lourie as chairman.

As media coverage intensified, the pressure on Westminster Conservatives was increasing – so much so that, on 22 February 1988, Peter Hartley, the man responsible for the decision to sell the cemeteries, dramatically resigned from the Council. He was not joined by his vice-chairman, Councillor Robert Davis.

Davis survived and steadily moved up the ranks to be chairman of the Planning Committee in the 1990s and Lord Mayor in 1995. By 2003 he was still on the City Council and one of the most powerful men in Westminster as Conservative chief whip, Cabinet member for Planning and Customer Services and close political ally of the leader, Simon Milton. Ironically, it was 26-year-old Milton who was subsequently elected in the Lancaster Gate ward on 14 April 1988, following Hartley's resignation.

Ominously for Labour, the Conservatives did not appear to suffer politically for the embarrassing 15p cemetery sale: Milton increased the Conservative share of the vote to more than 70 per cent.

On 13 June 1988 Bill Taylor's internal inquiry into the sale of the cemeteries conveniently singled out Hartley for criticism. It described him as being in the driving seat, and that 'during his journey a number of signals were ignored, the committee was not adequately informed and there were failures of communication between the driver and his passengers, the controlling Conservative group on the city council.'

The Council tried to cover up what had taken place. When we asked to see all the information considered by Taylor we were told that files containing sensitive details of the deals had been 'impounded'. In addition, vital passages of the evidence were missing from confidential transcripts we requested because, according to Council officers, the tape machinery used to record the four months of evidence malfunctioned. In particular, there were huge gaps in the transcripts of evidence given by George Touchard, director of Property Services at the time of the cemetery sales. It was during Touchard's evidence that it was alleged that letters had been taken out of the files and sensitive documents had been impounded because Conservative Councillors did not want Labour to see them. Unsurprisingly, Taylor's report recommended no disciplinary action against officers.

Later that year, on 4 November, John Magill, the district auditor, published his report on the sale of the cemeteries. His report was a damning indictment of the Council, which made uncomfortable reading for them:

> They [the Council] gave insufficient thought to their actions and those of the purchaser and were consequently outmanoeuvred by him at every turn. At no stage was there any comprehensive attempt made on behalf of the council to value the properties and graveyards . . . This was a remarkable state of affairs.
>
> Shortcomings flowed from the attitudes and culture current in Westminster at the time. This manifested itself in the poor com-

munications between officers and members and in particular in the
reluctance of officers to report what appeared to them to be facts
which would be unpalatable to members. In arriving at decisions,
relevant factors were inadequately considered or not considered at all,
and there were major weaknesses and errors in the implementation of
those decisions.

But, with typical arrogance and an unbelievable failure to see the
district auditor's obvious criticism of the way in which she ran the
City Council, Shirley Porter welcomed the report, which, she
claimed, 'nailed the smears and lies which have been circulated.
The auditor has found no evidence of fraud or corruption.'

More criticism of the Council was to follow a month later, on
7 December 1988, when the local government ombudsman, Dr
David Yardley, found the City Council guilty of maladminis-
tration over the sale of the three cemeteries. Yardley found that
the Council

clearly owed a moral obligation over and above their strict legal duties
in relation to those whose relatives and loved ones were buried in the
cemeteries . . . Members believed, or gave the impression they
believed, that some officers were intent on sabotaging their policy of
running the Council on more business-like lines.

Worse was to follow for the Conservatives when Magill started his
public interest hearings into the sale of the cemeteries on 19 July
1989. This inquiry followed our objection to the Council's
accounts. Held at the GLC-free County Hall, the hearings were
open to the public, and our case was put by Gavin Millar, a
Church Street councillor and a barrister at Doughty Street
Chambers. Millar set out the case against the Council with devastating simplicity. He told the district auditor that Conservative
councillors ignored 'repeated and clear advice from both Council
officers and cemetery experts' that the sale to private interests
would inevitably result in a deterioration of maintenance
standards and asset-stripping by the purchaser.

Magill published his public interest report on the sale of
Westminster's three cemeteries on 16 February 1990. He found

'imprudence, error of judgement, negligence and misconduct'. He also condemned the cemetery sale as 'unlawful and unauthorised' and 'to the detriment of ratepayers'. The report was also critical of the conduct of Hartley, chief executive Rodney Brooke and Touchard.

In dismissing our calls for her resignation, Porter again claimed she had done nothing wrong. She claimed:

> The report exonerates the council and myself, and to an amazing degree, it says in no way was I responsible. I regret what has taken place, but I really do feel the smear campaign waged by the opposition at great cost to the ratepayers has finished up in another report which says there was no wilful misconduct by any of the present officers and none of the councillors.

The storm of disapproval about the sale continued, however, with relatives continuing to harry the Council at every turn. Finally, on 29 June 1992, the City Council's Policy and Resources Committee agreed to buy back the three cemeteries it sold in 1987 for 15p. But this time the Council had to pay over £4 million and never recovered the valuable land and buildings which were sold with the cemeteries. It was a true national scandal. Yet it was just a taste of things to come as Porter plotted to cling on to power.

5

Blowing the whistle on 'Homes for Votes'

In 1988, opposition members on the Council raised questions about why the key/marginal wards were being monitored. There were deliberate attempts by officers to conceal the system of monitoring which had been established by giving deliberately misleading answers to proper questions from members of the minority party on the Council.

High Court 'Agreed Statement of Facts', 1997

As the impact of the designated sales policy began to bite, the Council's actions began to provoke questions across Westminster. In February 1988, Dr Richard Stone, a Bayswater GP, wrote to the district auditor to ask him to investigate why there were so many empty, boarded-up council flats on the Hallfield estate, in Bayswater. Dr Stone wrote to the district auditor because he was trying to help patients move into more suitable council accommodation – including an elderly widower with a heart complaint who was a prisoner in his fourth-floor flat.

Later Dr Stone explained what he saw. He said that he

started seeing steel doors going up on council homes. I began to wonder what was going on. Sadly the elderly widower died waiting for a new home. He probably would have died anyway. But the quality of life for that man was terrible. I was horrified he had not been rehoused. When I think of people living in bed and breakfast, I think how outrageous it was to keep homes empty and from those in housing and medical need.

For over eighteen months Shirley Porter and her colleagues kept the lid on details of their key wards election strategy and the way in which they were using Council money and Council staff to implement their 1990 election plans. Even though, as it was later revealed, the Conservatives meticulously recorded their plans using forests of paper, from May 1986 to early 1988 not one piece of paper fell into Labour hands. And this was despite our very robust and public opposition to the Council's designated sales policy.

However, in early 1988 that was to change dramatically when one solitary piece of paper from the Housing Department found its way to Neale Coleman. That one piece of paper explained exactly what was happening. On it was a list of Council housing sales analysed by 'key ward'. Officially, the Council did not have a key ward policy. Indeed, no wards were officially designated as key. However the list of wards in which housing sales were being monitored each month was explicit – the eight 'key wards' were Bayswater, Cavendish, Churchill, Hamilton Terrace, Little Venice, Millbank, Victoria and West End.

Coleman passed the Housing Department paper to me, and I wrote to Bill Phillips, the City Council's managing director, on 17 March 1988, demanding an explanation. I was seething with anger but tried my best to play it as dispassionately as possible:

> It has come to my attention that officers in the Housing Department are both allocating resources to and monitoring decisions in respect of Key Wards. I have no idea why officers should have selected these wards and why they should be classified as Key. The only explanation is that they are considered to be marginal by members of the Majority Party. I find it extraordinary that Council officers should be allocating resources and monitoring action on the basis of a secret political strategy.

For the next thirteen months, until the end of April 1989, I continued my correspondence with Phillips, but all I ever got from him were repeated denials that a key ward strategy existed. Indeed, the more I asked, the more Phillips and his colleagues denied that anything wrong was taking place.

On 22 March 1988, Phillips replied to me, emphatically denying that there was a key ward policy. In very robust terms he claimed:

> I must make it absolutely clear that it would be unacceptable for any officer to discharge his or her duties in a way which favoured a political party. I can assure you that Mr England [Graham England, director of Housing] has confirmed that resources are not being allocated per se into the wards which you identify.

But the district auditor was later to find:

> Mr Phillips knew that he and other officers (and members) were embarked on a plan of action to secure electoral advantage for the majority party, a course of action which he knew to be wrong. Mr Phillips therefore sought to obfuscate and to deceive Councillor Dimoldenberg as to what was happening.

On 29 March 1988, I replied to Phillips, but this time enclosing a copy of the Housing Department paper. I said that it was an 'extract from a report sent to Councillor Dutt and copied to Councillor Coleman [showing that] the Housing Department is indeed monitoring activity in respect of key wards and has been doing so for some time as is evidenced by the running total'. In addition, I made the point that

> no Council or Committee decisions have been made to agree the allocation of resources on this basis and I can only conclude that you and your colleagues are acting illegally. I think that you and Mr England owe my colleagues and me a public apology for the clear untruth which is contained in the final two sentences of third paragraph of your letter of 22nd March.

From then on, Porter and her colleagues, as well as all the Council officers involved, knew that they had been rumbled. In the following months they sought desperately to find an acceptable justification for the blatantly politically partisan policies they were implementing in the name of the Council. So, on 12 April 1988, the Chairmen's Group was informed that the Building Stable Communities (BSC) Members' Steering Group would consider a BSC monitoring report and a 'rationale for key wards' at its meeting of 28 April.

At that meeting, the Members' Steering Group decided that monitoring reports were needed to predict what the cumulative effect of BSC initiatives would be by October 1989, the date that the electoral registers would be drawn up for the 1990 elections. It was agreed that a one-page summary for each key ward would be prepared, showing progress on designated sales, together with a forecast for right-to-buy sales and planning permissions for luxury housing. In addition, each key ward was given a performance target. But they could not find a rationale for the key ward policy itself. The only rationale for the key wards was that they were marginal in electoral terms.

Sydney Sporle, director of Planning and Transportation, prepared a paper for the 28 April meeting entitled 'Building Stable Communities – Developing an Area Approach'. Unfortunately for Porter, the paper did not provide any rationale for the selection of the eight key wards; it simply looked at ways of going public on targeted wards. It was quickly agreed that the paper should not be a formal document and that each ward would be taken individually. Graham England's note of the meeting accurately described the hole that he and the Conservatives were in: 'Minority Party interest not easy to confirm just the 8 . . . Keep on dodging???'

By now, Phillips was taking even longer to reply to my letters. It took him nearly two months to reply to my 29 March letter and his response, dated 24 May 1988, was more of the same evasions. He wrote: 'I have seen no evidence to support the assertions made in your letter, and I take this opportunity to tell you that I do not purvey "clear untruths" to anybody.' Yet, three weeks earlier, on the weekend of 7 and 8 May 1988, Phillips was present at a chairmen's strategy weekend at Frimley Hall, Camberley, where the Conservatives discussed a BSC action plan, which included 'a summary of progress on the implementation of the initiative' setting out voter targets for each of the key wards. They were keen to ensure that the new voters were, according to Dr Michael

Dutt, vice-chairman of the Housing Committee, the 'right stuff'. Also, a 'Key Ward Analysis' report included a timeline, which summarised 'significant milestones' for the project. The 'significant milestone' for 1988 was identified as 'Defence of Key Wards under attack from Minority Party'.

The fact that we were on their trail was clearly a worry to the Conservatives, but Porter and her colleagues ploughed on regardless. At a Members' Steering Group meeting on 31 May 1988, the Conservatives agreed that Cavendish, St James's and West End were to be the priority areas, and bar charts were produced illustrating progress in each of the key wards.

Not content with Phillips's evasive replies I wrote to him again on 21 June 1988:

> You have yet to give me a satisfactory answer to why officers in the Housing Department are monitoring decisions on Designated Sales in respect of 'key' wards . . . I know that the Majority Party has selected the wards for party political reasons, but there is no justification for Council officers to serve these political ends using Council resources. I want to know – by return – what is going on; who sanctioned the action; when it is going to stop.

I sent a copy of this letter to the district auditor, John Magill, to alert him to what I believed to be unlawful activity by the Council. I followed this up on 7 July with a formal letter to Magill to ask that he issue a prohibition order under the Local Government Act 1988:

> As expenditure on these matters is unlawful and is likely to cause a loss or deficiency, I consider these matters to be of the utmost importance and I look to you to act in the public interest as a matter of urgency to stop the Majority Party using the Council machinery and professional officers for their own party political ends.

Two weeks later, on 22 July, Magill sent a brief and terse letter: 'As you will appreciate, the questions you raised with me are complex. As soon as I have had an opportunity to consider the matter in detail, I will be in touch with you again.' Disappointingly, Magill never did get back in touch with me about the Council's key wards. If he had started his investigations in July 1988 the Conservatives might have been stopped dead in their tracks. It was not until *Panorama* broadcast details of the Council's 'key wards' strategy and a formal objection was submitted almost one year later, on 19 July 1989, that the district auditor began to take action, despite these matters having been brought to his attention a full twelve months previously.

With the district auditor taking no interest at this stage, the Conservatives continued on their gerrymandering course and still looked for a way to explain why eight wards were 'key'. On 25 July 1988 England met with Dutt and discussed, according to England's notes of the meeting, 'explanation for eight wards', 'public audit . . . can we justify why eight were chosen?' and 'why did we pick them? Members will ask us'. England's action list as a result of the meeting included 'key wards – find defence of 8 wards'.

We increased the pressure on Porter and Phillips by briefing the press on what was happening at City Hall. Sarah Baxter of *Time Out* magazine was particularly interested in the story and called Phillips for his response to my claims that Council officers and Conservative councillors were in cahoots to rig the 1990 elections. Phillips dismissed the claims with lofty disdain – 'It would be totally unacceptable for any officer to discharge their duties in a way that favours political parties.' But, under pressure to explain exactly how the Council came up with the key ward policy, according to Baxter

> he initially suggested the decision to monitor key wards was taken by the housing committee, but when pressed, said he 'thought' it was agreed by the policy unit. He added that each chief officer had denied that they were channelling resources into particular areas and said that he had yet to be convinced that further inquiries were necessary. (*Time Out*, 3 August 1988)

On 25 August 1988, Matthew Ives, the City Solicitor, wrote an internal memo to his fellow chief officers to ask why the eight wards were chosen, by whom they were chosen and why they were regarded as key. He followed up his bland request for information with the extraordinary statement that 'it may be that, contrary to Councillor Dimoldenberg's expectations, there is an entirely innocent explanation for the use of the word "key" in this particular context'.

And despite Ives's request for an explanation from his colleagues, unsurprisingly, his questions were never answered. The constant questioning did, however, result in one small change in Porter's approach. After a chairmen's strategy weekend on 17 and 18 September 1988, all the papers were shredded in order to avoid any more leaks. At about the same time it was decided that in future BSC reports should be given orally rather than on paper.

This was followed up, on 3 October, by moves to remove any opportunity Labour councillors might have to get hold of Council papers on key ward matters. Phillips wrote a confidential memo to Sydney Sporle on the subject of 'BSC Monitoring', suggesting:

> I think it would be helpful to bear in mind . . . that sight of Steering Group reports may be sought by Members of the Council who are not members of the Steering Group. It could be argued by those other members that these are reports on progress on major Council policies and that they therefore have a need to see them in order to discharge their functions as Councillors. Unless papers are intended for wide circulation, could you please ensure that: (a) meetings of the Steering Group are given the status of informal, non-executive meetings; and (b) that the headings/format of papers produced for the Steering Group reflect this informal status.

This was a serious case of belt and braces. Not only did the key wards policy not exist, but the Council was taking action to ensure that all references to the non-existent policy would be kept away from the prying eyes of Labour councillors!

The Conservatives now put into play a series of dirty tricks operations. On 4 October, Porter wrote to Rodney Brooke, the Council's chief executive, to suggest that he should mount an inquiry into Peter Bradley, the deputy chief whip, and me. Porter's letter said:

I have today received the attached letter from a concerned resident. As you will see, it makes disturbing reading, raising as it does, important questions about the role of Councillors Dimoldenberg and Bradley within the City Council. Should I order a thorough inquiry? . . . Has Councillor Dimoldenberg ever formally reported to the Authority that he is touting for business using the fact that he is the Opposition Leader of the City Council? Do you think I should contact the Fraud Squad? Serious issues are at stake. Who knows, perhaps Councillor Dimoldenberg has been involved in numerous planning matters that have been dealt with by the Council in the last couple of years. I am very worried about this. It would not help the good name of the City if we had a major corruption case on our hands. But we must behave properly. Whatever the ending, the truth must out. There must be no cover ups. As you will see from the final paragraph, the sender of the letter asked for their name and address to be withheld and only revealed with their prior consent. I quite understand that if the charges they make are true they could face harassment of an awful kind.

Thankfully, Brooke was having none of Porter's games. He replied by return, on 5 October: 'There is no evidence from the papers sent to me that either Councillor Dimoldenberg or Councillor Bradley has misused his Membership of the Council. There is no offence in stating that a person is a Councillor as part of his curriculum vitae.'

The next opportunity for the Conservatives to smear us came the following week, at the Policy and Resources Committee meeting on the evening of 17 October. This time Conservative chief whip Barry Legg led the assault and Brooke was instructed to 'investigate the links of Dun & Bradstreet with two members of the Policy and Resources Committee, and Dun & Bradstreet's involvement in the sundry debtor work of the Council'.

Legg had produced an extract from the *Public Relations Consultants' Association Yearbook*, which listed the major clients of Good Relations (the company that Peter Bradley and I both worked for, which I had joined in February 1988). Neither of us worked on the Dun & Bradstreet account. Indeed, until Legg pointed it out, we were unaware that Dun & Bradstreet was a

Good Relations client. Legg thought he had scored a direct hit and was very pleased with himself, but he must have been terribly disappointed when, on 13 January 1989, Brooke reported to the Policy and Resources Committee on the 'potential pecuniary interests of Members of the Committee through relationships between the Council and Dun & Bradstreet Ltd', pointing out that 'no situation in which a pecuniary interest warrants disclosure has been found'. That, however, did not stop Porter's dirty tricks campaign, and one of the actions agreed at the Majority Party Strategy Weekend on 9 May 1989 was to 'neutralise Dimberg'.

At the same time, the pressure on the Conservatives and on Porter in particular was also mounting. In November 1988 news of an internal Conservative Party investigation began to surface. 'Lady Porter has the ability to turn even a minor problem into a national embarrassment,' according to one of her colleagues. Another added: 'There is a feeling that Lady Porter is personally responsible for much of the mud flung at us.'

Porter survived the Central Office investigation, no doubt by persuading the Conservative grandees that her removal would be seen as a big victory for Labour. It would also have also come as a huge relief for Conservative councils, councillors and MPs up and down the country, who were becoming increasingly tired of being compared with Porter's Westminster. The 15p cemeteries had quickly entered local government folklore.

With the new year barely underway, the Conservatives quickly returned to their stride. Future leader Simon Milton's growing involvement with Porter's plans was highlighted on 2 February 1989, when a strictly confidential note on the Planning and Development Committee's 'priorities for 1989' included the item 'Politicising the planning process – S. Milton/R. Davis to do this with Mark McGregor', with an instruction that 'summary needed of all activity in key wards'.

Meanwhile, Porter was still worried about the acres of bad publicity she and her Council were getting. So, in February 1989, she turned to the master, 'Mrs Thatcher's favourite PR man', Tim Bell, for help. Not only was Bell Margaret Thatcher's long-time confidant, but he was also my and Bradley's boss at Good Relations, one of his subsidiary companies! There was clearly an element of calculation in Porter's approach to Bell.

Bell assigned the job of advising Porter to one of his most experienced consultants, Alan Kilkenny. The *Sunday Times* columnist Valerie Grove related her experience of interviewing Porter on 19th February 1989:

> Before seeing Porter I had to submit a list of questions. 'I know you'll say who does she think she is, the Queen or something,' apologised the Westminster Council press officer, but my first question was unscheduled. Who was that man sitting with us at the table of the Mayfair restaurant? He was Alan Kilkenny from Lowe Bell Communications, but why was he here?
>
> 'He has come to the aid of the party,' declared Porter. 'The party being me.' She was faced, she explained, with an enormous personal attack, mounted by the leader of the opposition, Paul Dimoldenberg. 'As you know,' she said, 'he works for Good Relations, the PR company. He is using professional expertise to try to get me out. So I've got myself some professional expertise as well. This is my minder.' 'Paid for by me', she added, 'not the rates.'
>
> She handed the minder the menu. 'I'd like some salmonella please, and some of what's that other stuff? Listeria.' He ordered seaweed.

By now, Porter's problems were coming thick and fast and not even Bell's skills could halt the negative newspaper headlines. On 8 February Brooke resigned his post, ten months before his contract was due to expire. In return for a pay-off said to be in the region of £1 million, Brooke was obliged to agree that he would not, without written consent from the Council, 'disclose to any third party and information related to it in any way connected with the management of the Council'. He was the second chief executive to leave Westminster early since Porter took power in 1983.

For Brooke, this was a sad episode in an otherwise glittering local government career. On his appointment in January 1984 he was described by the Conservatives as 'a man highly regarded in his profession . . . of total and unquestioned integrity'. Talking about Brooke's departure, one senior Westminster Conservative observed: 'When Rodney joined he was viewed as the greatest thing since sliced bread. Then one day he said "no" to something Shirley wanted done and that was that' (*Evening Standard*, 17 January 1994).

Porter was fighting on so many fronts – against Labour, against many of her disgruntled Conservative colleagues, against the press and against some of her own senior City Hall staff. Could there possibly be anyone else left to fight? Time to bring on the residents of the Walterton and Elgin estates!

6

The battle of Walterton and Elgin

The over-riding objective of the Chairmen in the management of [Hermes and Chantry] Points became the defeat of the WECH Ltd [Walterton and Elgin Community Homes] bid. No adequate thought was given, nor adequate advice taken, in relation to the asbestos risk. I have to conclude that the real reason for the decision to accommodate homeless families in the Points was to assist the hoped-for defeat of the WECH bid; that the decision was . . . influenced by considerations of party advantage. Despite the availability of the clearest advice and instructions to the contrary, those acting on behalf of a public body repeatedly took risks, for a variety of reasons, with the health of people who ought to have been entitled to assume that such risks were not being taken.

> John Barratt, former chief executive of Cambridgeshire County Council, in his report 'The Management of Hermes and Chantry Points Given the Presence of Asbestos Materials', 25 March 1996.

The Walterton and Elgin estates had been the front line of the Conservative assault on Labour's north Paddington stronghold back in the autumn of 1985. Residents from the two former GLC estates were prominent at Housing Committee and Council meetings from 1985 onwards. They were led by Shirland Road resident Jonathan Rosenberg and his wife Jackie, who was elected as a Labour councillor for the Maida Vale ward in May 1986. Walterton and Elgin residents were a mix of young people who had moved into the area in the early 1980s, when the GLC made the unpopular flats available on a first-come-first-served basis, together with older long-standing residents such as Irene

Blackman, whose late husband Con had been a Labour councillor
in the 1960s and 1970s.

The Walterton and Elgin residents took on the Council – and
anyone who was remotely interested in collaborating with the
Council on the demolition and redevelopment of their homes –
with uncompromising vigour. In his book, *Rent Boy*, Pete May
described the innovative tactics employed by the Walterton and
Elgin Action Group (WEAG):

> WEAG's response to the council sell-off was both brilliant and
> amusing. A coach full of residents and journalists arrived
> unannounced at the offices of one of the potential developers and we
> told the flustered receptionist that we'd like to be consulted about our
> homes being sold. Then Rory McLeod, a folk singer who lived in
> Hermes Point, took out his acoustic guitar and led the throng in a
> chorus of WEAG's anthem 'Defending Our Homes'. Men in suits ran
> around like harried termites pursued by anteaters, bemused to find a
> mini-Glastonbury in their sanitised yuppie offices. (Pete May, *Rent
> Boy: How One Man Spent 20 Years Falling off the Property Ladder*,
> Mainstream, 2004)

Always looking for ways to outwit the Council, Jonathan
Rosenberg had come up with the novel idea of using Nicholas
Ridley's new 'Tenants' Choice' legislation, designed to enable
council tenants to escape from bad council landlords, as a way of
Walterton and Elgin tenants preventing the demolition of their
homes by becoming their own landlord. If the Walterton and
Elgin tenants were to succeed, they would become the first
tenants in the country to benefit from this latest piece of
Conservative privatisation. So, a new law designed to embarrass
poorly performing Labour councils was set to do exactly that to
Tory flagship Westminster.

Porter and her colleagues were rendered apoplectic by
WEAG's application to the Department of the Environment to
exercise Tenants' Choice – so much so that they began a new
programme of dirty tricks intended to scupper the WEAG bid.
On 17 January 1989 an informal meeting with chairmen agreed
that a paper needed to be prepared on 'options for obstructing the

WEAG bid, looking at all the possibilities, their advantages and their implications'.

It was not long before the Council began to take steps to foil the Walterton and Elgin residents by sending in workmen to smash up the empty flats, including the toilets. Often this resulted in the flooding of the flats below, where people were living. The Council had, in effect, declared war on its own tenants in an effort to stop them exercising their legal rights.

On 24 January, at another informal meeting of chairman, 26-year-old Councillor Simon Milton became lead member for dealing with the WEAG Tenants' Choice bid. A confidential report on the current status of the bid advised that 'the most immediate way to stop the transfer is for the Housing Corporation not to approve WECH [Walterton and Elgin Community Homes] as a landlord'. The paper argued that it was vital to 'destroy the financial viability of the transfer so that the Corporation revokes approval or WECH abandons its bid'. In terms of Council action, the paper advised that the Council should 'fill up empty flats on tower blocks to limit JR [Jonathan Rosenberg]'s decanting options and stop him using them as a source of income by letting for homeless families'.

May describes the campaign waged by the Conservatives to stop the transfer to WECH:

> There were rumours of dirty tricks when a group called 'Westminster Residents Against Takeover' emerged. The only three members of WRAT ready to be identified were two former tenants who had bought their council flats and one man who no longer lived on the estate but had been a member of Harrow Road ward Conservative Party.
>
> After a little research, it soon became apparent that the address given by WRAT on its leaflets did not exist. Appropriately, WRAT then seemed to go underground, and one of its members was reduced to putting this message on his answer machine: 'This is a private number and has nothing to do with WRAT'. No one knew who was really behind WRAT, but many had their suspicions.

Porter's attempt to wreck the WECH bid was put into a higher gear on 21 February 1989, when the Chairmen's Group decided to rehouse homeless families in asbestos-ridden flats in Hermes and Chantry Points, on the Elgin estate. There is little doubt that Hermes and Chantry Points were dangerous. Indeed, Graham Farrant, the City Council's assistant divisional director (Maintenance), wrote an MSc thesis in 1986, which stated:

> It is considered that these two blocks . . . may provide the greatest potential for asbestos release within residential accommodation in Britain. In particular, easy access to the loose lagging in the common parts and the degree of vandalism encountered in these blocks give rise to concern among the tenants as to their exposure.

The decision to house families in the two tower blocks was subsequently the subject of two separate inquiries, one by a former chief executive of Cambridgeshire County Council, John Barratt, in 1994 and the other by the district auditor, John Magill, in 2004. In his 2004 Public Interest Report, Magill said:

> The decision to place homeless households in the points was unlawful. The decision was taken and implemented without proper authority and . . . as with many other decisions taken at the time, it was taken by the Chairmen's Group and implemented by officers. The decision was influenced by irrelevant considerations which were taken into account including the (secret) policy of certain leading Members at the time to defeat the exercise by WECH of its statutory rights.

Milton later tried to explain his involvement in the decision to place families in asbestos-ridden flats. He told the *West End Extra* on 6 February 2004:

> I was the youngest member of the Council and had been a councillor for just eight months. As far as I was concerned that was how things operated. No way could anyone, who is elected to the Council having never served before, be in a position to know how things operated. I had been invited to attend the Chairmen's Group to be an assistant and pass information from the group to the whole Conservative Group. Officers said that these buildings had been lying empty, were

being vandalised, and we had this huge housing problem and why don't we put these people in there.

Milton, however, was being modest. Before his election to the Council in 1988, he was already a seasoned political activist, who had been the youngest-ever chairman of the Cambridge University Conservative Association in the early 1980s, when it had over a thousand members. Although he was not involved with the genesis of 'Building Stable Communities', by January 1989, just a few months after his by-election victory, and throughout much of that year, he was attending strategy week-ends and 'informal' meetings of the Chairmen's Group. At these meetings there was routine discussion of the monitoring of key ward targets.

Thankfully, the Council's attempts to derail WECH's plans to exercise Tenants' Choice failed. In late March 1989 Walterton and Elgin Community Homes Ltd became Britain's first approved landlord under the 1988 Housing Act. In October 1991, WECH finally made history and voted itself out of Council control. The ballot, which had an 82 per cent turn-out, was the first ever held under the government's Tenant's Choice legislation. Some 72 per cent of residents voted for WECH to take control from the Council and in the following April 921 flats on the Elgin and Walterton Estate passed into the ownership of WECH.

It was not until August 1994 that there was a proper inquiry into the dirty tricks, when Bill Roots, the Council's new chief executive, called in the district auditor to extend his inquiry into the Council's housing policy. Roots called Magill in, less than three weeks after taking up his post, after reading a confidential 24-page report drawn up on his instruction into the way the Walterton and Elgin estates were transferred to tenants' control. The report, by John Barratt, said the Council had a legal case to answer over the way its officers sought to block the bid by tenants to take over their homes. Barratt found evidence to suggest that Council officers had been under orders from Conservative councillors to raise as many obstructions as possible to stop tenants.

Barratt also discovered evidence to show that the Council had written to the Housing Corporation suggesting that the tenants were not competent to run the estate and advising against funds being provided. Other delays and obstructions meant that, even though government policy favoured this type of scheme, it had taken tenants six years of hard negotiation with the Council before they could set up a company to take over the estate. On 25 March 1996, nearly two years after it had been commissioned, the Council finally published Barratt's report, 'The Management of Hermes and Chantry Points Given the Presence of Asbestos Materials'. The report found that the Council's former leaders had 'erected a hypocritical smokescreen', and 'it is abundantly clear that the bad conditions of the Points were known to the political decision-makers, and that asbestos was a major factor'.

Thankfully, two years later, in January 1997, an independent inquiry commissioned by WECH and the City Council found that the health risks to residents was very low. The Council and WECH commissioned Professor Julian Peto of the Institute of Cancer Research to examine potential medical risks. His report concluded that there was only about a one-in-twenty chance that a single extra cancer would eventually occur among the 3,000 former residents of the flats. Peto said that, in view of the very low extra overall risk, there was no special reason for the former residents to have regular health checks.

7
Panorama breaks the story

I remember vividly how the Dame Shirley Porter marathon began. The libel QC who was advising our BBC *Panorama* programme . . . had ploughed his way through piles of internal Conservative Party papers. Drawing heavily on his Turkish cigarette, he drawled: 'This is obviously true.'

John Ware, *Guardian*, 10 May 1999

Panorama has since the 1950s set the agenda for national discussion and debate. So, when in late March 1989 I received a phone call from *Panorama* producer Mark Killick telling me that he wanted to discuss Westminster's housing policies and the Conservatives' 'key ward' strategy, I jumped at the opportunity. This was just what was needed to expose what was happening at City Hall.

Killick and *Panorama* reporter John Ware took little time to decide to follow up the story and begin interviews. Renegade Conservatives such as Patricia Kirwan, former Conservative chairman of the Housing Committee, and Tony Prendergast needed little persuasion to talk on the record. In May 1989, *Panorama* even got access to the AGM of the Cities of London and Westminster Conservative Association, where Shirley Porter tried unsuccessfully to defeat the incumbent chairman, former councillor Iain Walker. Porter's candidate, Councillor Andrew Greystoke, was massively defeated by 151 votes to 27 and it was all recorded on camera.

Porter wanted to defeat Walker and replace him with Greystoke in order to sack the Conservative Party agent, Donald Stewart, who had opposed her plan to directly employ five political activists to campaign and mount dirty tricks against Labour councillors in the key wards.

The *Panorama* team put in a huge amount of work analysing all the Council reports and other documents that we supplied them. On 19 July 1989, the same day as the district auditor was holding his public interest hearings into the cemeteries sale, *Panorama* broadcast its exposé of the Council's illegal 'Homes for Votes' strategy. Kirwan, the star witness, told *Panorama*:

> There was a breakfast meeting in Lady Porter's room [after the 1986 elections] with the leader of one of the other Conservative boroughs in inner London at which he made the suggestion that what had happened in his borough was what Westminster ought to be doing, and that home ownership [would attract] a certain type of person – upwardly mobile Conservative-type voters in specific key areas to ensure the vote went up. I well remember Shirley [Porter] saying: 'Listen here, all of you, whenever you see that word 'stable communities' it means we're going to try and win that ward.'

Panorama set out the facts in stark, simple terms. In the key wards 81 per cent of empty homes were designated for sale, while in other parts of Westminster only 36 per cent were. Even that was a revision of the original plan to designate all homes for sale in the key wards. Kirwan told *Panorama* that the subsequent modification of the plans, prompted by a warning from the director of Housing, was 'a cosmetic exercise to make it look like it wasn't a complete fix'.

The *Panorama* programme featured a number of ex-Council employees, including a former chief press officer, Louise Richards, who said of Porter: 'She could be very difficult to work for. Once you did not remain "flavour of the month", as we used to say, she could drop you and demoralise you and make your working life very, very difficult.' Former director of Property Services George Touchard revealed: 'I have never had to work in a climate like I worked in here, and I've dealt with some pretty difficult socialist councils.'

The *Panorama* programme revealed that the Conservatives had compiled secret dossiers on all Labour councillors and their families, including details of personal relationships, property holdings and financial and other interests. Prendergast explained his reaction on hearing about the secret dossiers: 'I was horrified. I just thought it was dirty tricks.'

That day, twelve Westminster residents, led by Neale Coleman, Peter Bradley and Dr Richard Stone, submitted an objection to the City Council's accounts to the district auditor, John Magill. Further objections were later made by Coleman on 8 November 1989. Nearly nine years later Magill explained his initial reaction to receiving the objection and the implications it had on the conduct and actions of Conservative councillors and senior Council officers:

> I had worked with all these people as their auditor for some years. I found it very difficult to start from the position that these people – when they denied it – were not actually telling me the truth. It was really quite late on in the inquiry before I became persuaded that some of these people were lying to me. (*Times*, 18 March 1998)

This was not the reaction of a man who had already made up his mind, as the Conservatives and their apologists were later to claim.

The response to the *Panorama* programme was massive and immediate, both in the media and within City Hall. In particular, the programme sparked off more inquiries into the political activists hired by Porter to undertake her dirty tricks operations. One Conservative councillor admitted: 'A number of us are very concerned about these people. They are now frequently attending private meetings. We don't know who is paying them. If you try to bring the subject up it immediately brings the spotlight on you as being anti-Shirley Porter.' A Conservative Party official said: 'There is concern that a shadow organisation has been set up using outside activists. What is unusual is the scale on which people have been brought in and individually funded.'

Within City Hall, the Conservatives and Council officers desperately tried to cover their tracks. For example, charts presented to the BSC Members' Steering Group from 28 July 1989 onwards recorded sales for all twenty-three wards in the City; not just the eight key wards. In addition, staff in the Housing Department were instructed that in future monitoring reports, wards should be listed in alphabetical order (previously the eight key wards had always come first). A month later, on 22 August 1989, Bill Phillips, Matthew Ives, Graham England and the new deputy City Solicitor, Colin Wilson, met. England's notes set out the situation very clearly. Under the heading 'legality' he wrote: 'Unlawful motive – selection of estates by members – discussed with MD and City Solicitor who consider current policy to be legally dead.'

Meanwhile, the cost of the Council's designated sales and key ward policies was beginning to mount. With hundreds of empty unsold flats in the key wards, by September 1989 the cost was estimated to be nearly £3 million a year, while temporary accommodation for the homeless was costing £6.6 million a year.

Unsurprisingly, the Council publicly refused to admit that anything wrong had taken place. On 27 November 1989, Phillips wrote to the district auditor, setting out the Council's formal response to the objection to the Council's accounts. The letter, drafted for Phillips by Wilson, completely rejected the objectors' allegations. 'The City Council rejects the allegations of unlawfulness which have been made,' was the unabashed response.

Wilson was also responsible for drafting Phillips's further response to the district auditor on the objectors' allegations in a letter sent on 1 May 1990. In that letter, the Council made it clear that it did not accept

> that the 'obvious and overwhelming inference' from the documents and from the eventual selection of properties is [that] the predominant consideration in selecting properties was party electoral advantage. No officer time was devoted to serving electoral ends and all information supplied at the request of members was relevant to the proper discharge of the City Council's functions. The fact that some or all of this information may have also been relevant or helpful to politicians from a political or electoral point of view cannot render the costs incurred by the Council in preparing papers which are otherwise perfectly legitimate *ultra vires* and unlawful as alleged and neither is there in my view any evidence of wilful misconduct.

The Council's legal defence of its activities would later come to be comprehensively overturned.

8

The poll tax fiddle and the 1990 City Council elections

[Conservative Party chairman Kenneth] Baker had gambled his somewhat ragged reputation as a packaging whiz on concentrating resources on the Conservatives' three low poll tax councils: Bradford (£276), Westminster (£195) and Wandsworth (£148) . . . Similarly he decided to take the principle head-on with the 'Conservatives Cost You Less' slogan. Hold two of the three flagships, the argument went, and he would be able to vindicate the tax.

Guardian, 5 May 1990

The 1990 City Council elections were always going to be hard fought, given the Conservatives' small majority. The Conservatives, however, feared that the government's poll tax proposals would provide the mortal blow and end their unbroken control of City Hall.

The mood in the Labour camp was very positive. We were running two very strong campaigns in the Cavendish and St James's wards. I had decided to move from the safe Labour Harrow Road to stand in the Cavendish ward and had been putting a lot of time and effort over the previous two years into taking up local casework. I was joined by Daniel Carlen, who had lived in Marylebone all his life, and his partner Hilary Allen, a nurse. On top of the local casework, we delivered thousands of local leaflets, organised petitions and ran two stalls each Saturday morning – one in Great Titchfield Street and the other in Marylebone High Street. As the campaign reached its climax I revisited hundreds of the residents I had made contact with over the previous few years to renew the contact and to ask if they would sign our election nomination forms. Nobody refused to sign.

In the St James's ward the story was similar. Allan Wylie moved from his Labour Churchill ward to lead the charge and he was joined by Pimlico resident Charlie Smith. Labour canvassers were everywhere, including Buckingham and St James's Palaces, where staff in the Royal Mews were liable for the poll tax, after never having had to pay rates.

On top of the intense local campaigning, the negative press stories exposing the continuing fiascos at City Hall produced a steady stream of background noise. The *Financial Times* wrote that the Labour opposition was 'sane and sensible'. The Labour pollster Phillip Gould, a Bayswater resident, carried out focus group research which confirmed that Shirley Porter was seen as 'arrogant and out of touch' with ordinary voters. We announced that the new Lord Mayor would be the veteran Harrow Road councillor and part-time taxi-driver Joe Glickman. Quietly, I sounded out City Treasurer David Hopkins to ask if he would take over as acting chief executive following the elections. He agreed without a moment's hesitation.

But the Conservatives realised that the poll tax would be the decider and did everything they could to keep it as low as possible. Just a few months before polling day, in March 1990, the City Council announced a poll tax of £195, the second lowest in the country. A year earlier the projected poll tax had been £429. However, successful lobbying by the company GJW on behalf of the Council persuaded the government to increase the amount of grant that the Council received, thereby enabling it to substantially reduce the poll tax.

The GJW campaign was targeted at key ministers such as the Agriculture Minister, John Gummer, who was thought to be particularly conscious that with safety nets a number of high-spending Labour London boroughs would get off the hook. GJW also produced a paper entitled 'Electoral Disaster: The Effects of Safety Netted Community Charge on Some Households in the City of Westminster', which went to Gummer and his colleagues in government. It specifically referred to the effects on 'marginal wards, like Cavendish and Little Venice' and on 'identified, aspiring Conservative voters'. It concluded that 'the electoral consequences are bound to be adverse' and included a number of tables which 'examine the financial impact on some of these groups in the two most marginal wards in the City'. The paper warned that 'such voters are the heart of the Cavendish Ward and are clearly essential to Conservative hopes to hold the City Council'.

The result of this lobbying was a huge increase in the grant received by Westminster. Nobody could work out quite how the figures were calculated, but there was much speculation that the Council's entitlement was deliberately 'miscalculated' to hand the Conservatives an extra £6.3 million.

The extent of the Conservative lobbying of Government was revealed when confidential Council papers were leaked to the Labour Party headquarters just a few days before the May 1990 elections. At a hastily arranged press conference, Labour's election coordinator, Jack Cunningham MP, demanded a full inquiry and accused the Conservatives of a 'squalid political exercise to keep down the poll tax in Westminster'.

Cunningham laid into the Council:

Yesterday morning Lady Porter told journalists: 'I've not had any lobby firm. We've not hired any firm and we've not paid any money to anyone to lobby.' Later, a spokesman for Lady Porter amended her statement and said that the lobbying had indeed taken place but 'was paid for by Westminster Conservative supporters'. On last evening's BBC TV news Lady Porter confirmed the change of line and said there had been lobbying 'without ratepayers' money'. On ITN's *News at Ten* she contradicted herself again, saying: 'Westminster has never employed professional lobbyists.' However, Mr Bill Phillips, managing director of Westminster City Council, has now contradicted Lady Porter and confirmed that Westminster City Council itself had indeed engaged the lobbyists GJW, for a six month contract at a fee of over £9,000 in September 1988.

As election day dawned, the predictions pointed to a close result. On 3 May 1990 the *Times* reported:

Tory candidates in Westminster are coming across wealthy voters unhappy at the benefits they receive from the change from rates to the poll tax. Both Cavendish and St James's are being vigorously fought by the parties and canvassed with an intensity more usual in a general election. Conservatives are now on their sixth canvass in St James's. On council estates, they always hope to hear musical doorbells, believing that a singing doorbell normally means they are Conservative.

And the 'singing doorbells' certainly delivered for the Conservatives when the votes were counted. Overall, the Conservatives increased their majority on the City Council from four to thirty as Labour lost twelve seats and Lois Peltz, the sole Independent councillor, was defeated in the West End ward. Labour casualties included me (despite us getting the highest-ever Labour vote in the Cavendish ward) and the deputy Labour leader, Neale Coleman, who was defeated in Maida Vale.

'One hundred and ninety five, that's the focus of our campaign, one hundred and ninety five,' a 'boisterously confident' Donald Stewart, Conservative Party agent proclaimed, just days before polling day. And, would you believe it, the Conservatives won seven out of the eight key wards, with only Millbank retaining its three Labour councillors.

9

The district auditor's investigations begin

> I knew all these people and had worked closely with them, so when I started getting documents which suggested there may have been something untoward, my starting point wasn't that here was a major investigation.
>
> It took quite a while to realise that there was something here. I wasn't helped in that documents weren't provided. We had to drag them out. Then we dug out more and had to go back to re-interview people.
>
> John Magill, district auditor, *Business Age*, July 1998

In the weeks leading up to the elections, I knew that we would not win. During March, my door-to-door canvassing made it crystal clear that the low £195 poll tax had already secured many former 'undecided' votes for the Conservatives. The Cavendish ward, where I was a candidate, was right on the border with Labour Camden and the Conservative election message was devastatingly effective: they simply posted the Conservative Westminster £195 poll tax figure with the Labour Camden figure of double that amount. For the ordinary voter the message was extremely potent and we did not stand a chance.

Election day itself was gloriously warm and sunny and people flocked to the polls. For the first time in my experience there were long queues at the polling stations at 8.00 a.m. and I recognised many of those waiting to vote, including the former Liberal MP Clement Freud, who increased my confidence by admitting that he had voted for us. For the next twelve hours and more we ran round the ward knocking on doors and telephoning the Labour 'promises' to urge them to come out and vote. But, as we tallied up the details of those who had voted, it soon became clear that the Conservatives had done a very good job of getting out their supporters, too.

Instead of the usual turn-out in the mid thirties, on which we had made our calculations, it was over 50 per cent. And so, despite securing the best ever Labour vote in the Cavendish ward, Daniel Carlen, Hilary Allen and I were defeated by more than 500 votes. The story was the same all over Westminster. In St James's, Labour went down by more than 300 votes and in Bayswater by a similar number. In Churchill, the Conservatives turned a Labour majority of more than 100 into a Conservative majority of around 400. And in Maida Vale, a healthy Labour majority of more than 500 disappeared and was replaced by a Conservative majority of around 100. In the West End ward, which the Independent councillor Lois Peltz had represented since 1978, the Conservatives triumphed by more than 300 votes, while in Hamilton Terrace, where the SDP–Liberal Alliance had come within 150 votes of victory in 1986, the Conservatives piled up a majority of more than 700.

The much reduced Labour Group met on Sunday 6 May at the Council House, and Andrew Dismore was elected leader, with Peter Bradley and Jenny Edwards, newly elected councillor for Church Street, elected as joint deputy leaders. But despite their election victory, the Conservatives could not stop the district auditor.

John Magill continued to delve deeper into the murky working of the Council. Between January and April 1991, he made a series of visits to City Hall to inspect more documents. And he made further extensive requests for documents in autumn 1991. However, Porter and Co. did not make life easy for him. As Magill later wrote in his report:

> Having regard to my wish to arrange interviews in a particular order, the progress of the interviews was hampered by a delay on the part of some prospective interviewees in responding to requests for interviews and by the apparent reluctance of some interviewees to attend for interview. On two separate occasions, I employed enquiry agents to trace the whereabouts of one interviewee.

Indeed, delays in the auditor's report became a continuing feature over the next five years, with Shirley Porter and her colleagues always quick to absolve themselves entirely for the slow progress. Council claims that they were cooperating fully with Magill were shown to be worthless in June 1993, when Magill mounted a raid on the Council to seize documents that it had previously refused to divulge.

In a letter to Neale Coleman, Magill revealed:

> I decided to visit council offices to examine more files for the period mid 1986 to late 1989, starting with the policy unit and managing director's office. During this visit, I was told by more than one person that documents had been shredded by a previous employee. This may be entirely innocent and the documents may not have been connected with designated sales but, in my mind, there was at least a possibility that some of the documents shredded might have been connected with designated sales.

Later, in 1998, Magill gave a number of interviews in which he admitted that twelve months into his investigation he effectively had to start again. People he had interviewed made reference to files that couldn't be found or did not exist. So he decided to visit the Council offices unannounced.

> The raid yielded a wealth of incriminating evidence. The search led to 'muniments', the vast filing area under Victoria Street that houses records. The departed head of the policy unit left his papers in a green filing cabinet, but it was nowhere to be found. Descending to muniments, Mr Magill thought he had hit the jackpot. 'I opened this huge metal door, and right in front of me was this battered old green filing cabinet, and I thought, this is my lucky day. I was almost trembling as I went up to open it.' His elation was short-lived. 'There was nothing in it. It was the wrong one. We searched high and low, and never found any of his papers.' (*Times*, 18 March 1998)

Despite the continuing scandal at Westminster, Porter got her reward from the new Prime Minister, John Major, for holding on to the Council at the May elections. In the New Year's Honours on 1 January 1991 she was made a Dame Commander of the Order of the British Empire (DBE) for 'services to local government'. This supplanted her previous title of 'Lady Porter', which she acquired when her husband Leslie was knighted in 1983. On collecting her honour, she remarked, without a trace of irony, that it was 'nice to have a title of one's own'.

Later that month Porter announced her own demise – but on her terms. On 20 February she stood down as leader of the Council and let it be known that she had 'agreed to let my name go forward for Lord Mayor in May'. She said she now wanted to promote new initiatives, including some on a Europe-wide basis to tackle the problems of litter and inner city environmental decay.

But still the fall-out from the 'Homes for Votes' scandal continued. In mid-July 1991 the Council called in the Fraud Squad to investigate purchases of council flats under the designated sales policy. According to the *Guardian*:

> In a recent case, a barman in a public house in Covent Garden, who was already living in a flat above a restaurant belonging to the pub, applied for and bought a council flat off Drury Lane. In another case, a resident porter in a block of flats owned by the Church Commissioners applied for and bought a council flat, even though he had stated on his application that a flat 'goes with my job'. In both cases, the council apparently failed to make the applicants sign a statutory declaration that they intended to move into the flats when they had completed the sale. (*Guardian*, 11 July 1991)

More bad news was to follow in June 1992, when it was revealed that a charity close to Porter had paid almost £100,000 to the public relations company which ran the Conservative group's re-election campaign. A letter from the Charity Commission to Labour councillor Peter Bradley revealed:

> The trustees of the Foundation [for Business Responsibilities] themselves determined that some of the payments made to Marketforce Communications Ltd in 1989 and 1990 could not be wholly justified in relation to the work undertaken by the company on behalf of the

foundation. The trustees had therefore decided that all sums paid to Marketforce should be reimbursed to the trustees regardless of whether some of the payments could be justified.

The Charity Commission inquiry concluded that the trustees of the Foundation for Business Responsibilities 'had not at all times maintained sufficiently close supervision over their staff, with the result that certain unauthorised payments had been made out of the charity's income'. This unwelcome news forced the foundation to repay the money and escape sanction from the Charity Commissioners. Porter, however, was not so lucky when Magill published his provisional findings.

10

The district auditor's provisional 'Homes for Votes' report

That there was something rotten at Westminster council was well known at least five years ago, but nothing was done. In 1988 both the District Auditor and the local ombudsman produced damning reports into the council's sale for a token 15p of three cemeteries and valuable adjacent land – all to save annual costs of £406,000.

'Dame Shirley', we commented in December 1988, 'has become an embarrassment to Westminster, to London and to the Conservative Party, and she should go.' Sadly for all three, she did not accept this advice until last year. The District Auditor concluded that 'the electoral advantage of the majority party was the driving force behind the policy of increased designated sales'. That amounted to gerrymandering, which he described as 'a disgraceful and improper purpose' – and unlawful. The verdict could scarcely be more crushing.

Independent, 14 January 1994

On 11 February 1993 Shirley Porter dramatically resigned from the City Council. After her year as Lord Mayor she had become less and less involved in the affairs of the Council. The threat of surcharge was certainly right at the top of her mind and those of the rest of the Council. Just a few weeks before Porter's resignation, on 2 January 1993, Mark Baylis, the City Council's head of communications, prepared a report on the recommended public relations response to the expected 'highly critical report on designated sales, with all the main players either censured or criticised'.

Baylis advised the Council's senior officers to

> expect a big splash on the day, repeated in the Sunday papers, followed by a rapid loss of interest. It will occasionally re-emerge, for example when Jack Straw mentions the subject in Parliament or when it is discussed by the Council. In other words it will become a running sore rather than a national scandal.

Oh, how wrong he was to be!

The recommended strategy included the proposal that the Council should 'neither admit nor hint that we acknowledge any wrongdoing', with 'Merv [Montacute, who had succeeded Bill Phillips as managing director in February 1991] to be the council spokesman at officer level, Simon Milton at political level'. Getting the window dressing right was also important, and Baylis advised that it would be a good idea to 'call a Council meeting to show our concern for propriety'.

Baylis's recommended tactics on the day advised that one of the priorities should be

> to project it as ancient history. When anticipating the possibility of a public hearing, after five years and a million pounds, the auditor may now want to hold a series of public hearings. We should consider our response to this scenario and, at the least, express our surprise or disappointment. The Council's tactics ought to draw attention discretely to the passage of time since the alleged events took place. This has two advantages: 1) it raises a question over the report's validity; 2) it places it in the past.

And, in a revealing set of briefing notes for media questions, Council spokesmen were advised to concentrate on presentation rather than content: 'The overall impression created in an interview is far more important than its intellectual content. Our tone must be totally positive. We represent an extremely successful authority and there is no need to be apologetic.'

Finally, when asked the $64,000 question, on key wards, the advice displayed the Council's total contempt for the auditor's inquiry. As Baylis explained: 'There may be questions about how the key wards were chosen and why they had to be specially monitored. Most tricky of all, why these eight wards differed from those identified by [Victor] Hausner.'

Baylis's recommended response revealed the depths to which the Council had sunk:

> Officers involved at the time were unable to give clear explanations, but felt the choice made some sense in that they were all in or around the Central Activity Zone where the threat to residential communities was the greatest. Again, we should stress that we are not contradicting the auditor, but point out that there were perfectly legitimate reasons for monitoring certain key wards. Nonetheless, it appears that no one at City Hall knows why certain wards were chosen, and it would be unwise for spokesmen to pretend that they do.

So there you have it. Nobody knows why the Council was spending public money on supporting the Conservatives and it is just as big a mystery to us at it is to you.

After Porter's resignation, her successor, David Weeks, was next to go. In July 1993, Weeks was forced to step down as Council leader after a major row with Montacute, following an April raid on Weeks' City Hall office, where 'begging letters' to Council contractors for financial contributions to Conservative coffers were found. With Weeks's departure, the 31-year-old Milton took over as acting leader of the Council.

Despite the best efforts of Porter and her colleagues to put obstacles in the way of Magill's efforts to track down the evidence, the district auditor ploughed on with dogged determination. His big breakthrough came when Simon Mabey, a former chairman of the Social Services Committee and a member of the Chairmen's Group, handed him a complete set of 'Homes for Votes' files, revealing a series of incriminating documents that had hitherto evaded Magill's forensic investigations. Mabey, an accountant with City firm Smith and Williamson, was Westminster's Lord Mayor in 1989/90. Unluckily for the Conservatives, he had kept every scrap of paper detailing every step taken by Porter and Co. in preparation for the 1990 Council elections. He handed the lot over to Magill.

Mabey's documents confirmed Magill's suspicions that incriminating evidence had been shredded and gave a fresh impetus to his enquiry. Armed with the papers, Magill returned to the Council offices and began a thorough search for copies which had escaped the shredder, including a painstaking check of the entire underground storage area containing many thousands of archived files. Later, when the Conservatives heard that Mabey had turned Queen's Evidence, he and his wife were shunned by his former colleagues even though they remain Conservative Party members and Bayswater residents.

Magill was also assisted by the evidence of Jeremy Sullivan QC, the City Council's counsel, which revealed that Sullivan did not see a copy of the final report to the Housing Committee which approved the designated sales policy. A draft was sent to Sullivan which he did approve but, according to him, was 'different in a number of substantial respects' from the final version. In his evidence to Magill, Sullivan was asked how he would react if the Council had said:

> The majority party nearly lost the last election and since then they have been talking about targeting marginal wards. We are collecting data on these eight wards, we are talking about designating all the properties in those eight wards and that was the sort of background flavour; what is your view of that?

Sullivan told Magill: 'I would have said: "It is unlawful." '

Sullivan did not see another key report – 'Westminster Housing and Economic Study' – which was commissioned by the Council from the economic consultants PA Cambridge. The report made clear that in 1987 there was a serious and worsening homeless problem in Westminster. It said: 'Housing problems for the most vulnerable groups are getting worse, an impression confirmed by the continuing high level of homelessness.' In his interview with Sullivan, Magill showed him the two volumes of the report, to discover if he had been asked to read it. Sullivan replied: 'I think I should have a fit if I had been asked to do that. I certainly was not. I am not sure whether I have ever been asked to read that, even in preparation for the judicial review proceedings.'

After five years' investigation, on 13 January 1994, the district auditor published his provisional report in a blaze of publicity, involving TV cameras, uniformed security guards and a yard-high pile of files. Just prior to publication, both Matthew Ives, City Solicitor, and Montacute announced their resignations from the Council. On top of that, on the eve of publication, John Magill was faced with a tricky legal problem when he was given independent legal advice that he could be sued by Porter and Barry Legg MP if he published the full text of his 700-page report in advance of a public hearing later in the year. The prospect of further delay in publishing the auditor's report was too much for Council deputy leader Simon Milton. He complained: 'Some senior people have waited four years subject to smear and innuendo for this report to be published. It is now outrageous that this will not happen because it will only fuel the present problem' (*Guardian*, 12 January 1994).

Happily for Milton and his concerned Conservative colleagues, that particular legal problem was overcome and the auditor's report was published the following day. Magill's provisional findings were that Porter and others were engaged in unlawful activity and concluded:

> Both the decision to increase the number of designated sales and the selection of the properties designated for sale were influenced by an irrelevant consideration, namely the electoral advantage of the majority Party . . . My provisional view is that the Council was engaged in gerrymandering, which I am minded to find is a disgraceful and improper purpose, and not a purpose for which a local authority may act.
>
> No local housing authority acting reasonably would adopt a policy, the anticipated consequences of which were that the number of homeless households placed in temporary accommodation would increase by 172 each year and that the net revenue costs to the council would increase by over £1.5 million in each succeeding year.

The response from the Council was straight out of Mark Baylis's recommended denial strategy. The Council leader, Miles Young, told the press that many of the district auditor's findings would be 'vigorously contested'. Weeks claimed: 'We have done nothing wrong and we have no regrets. We didn't lumber in without taking careful legal advice, and the bottom line is this policy was very popular with Westminster residents' (*Daily Mail*, 14 January 1994).

Young and Weeks were later joined by the former Westminster Conservative councillor Teresa Gorman MP, who had lost her Millbank ward seat in 1986, and who now led the attack on the integrity of the district auditor and his advisers in Parliament. Gorman claimed in the House of Commons on 26 January 1994 that Touche Ross, Magill's firm, 'by prolonging this inquiry over many years, have claimed £250 an hour for every hour served by Mr Magill'. She then told MPs that among those who helped prepare the auditor's report was Tony Childs, who now worked for the Audit Commission, claiming that he was 'no stranger to controversy'. She said: 'He was formerly the solicitor and adviser to the hard-left council at Greenwich for a number of years, during which time that council was ill advised not to set a rate and was eventually overruled by the district auditor.'

Gorman accused Childs of being 'highly politically motivated' and said that he had helped to produce a report 'peppered with emotive language' and 'quotable quotes' for newspapers. Unfortunately for the Conservatives, Patricia Kirwan weighed in with a devastating put-down of the entire 'Homes for Votes' plot:

> I said financially it was batty, politically it would not work, legally it was doubtful and I thought it was indefensible. The reason I worked against the designated sales policy was because I felt it failed on all those counts . . . That is why I tried to stop it and why I resigned from the Council. (*Daily Mail*, 14 January 1994)

Meanwhile, Labour piled on the pressure, with their leader, John Smith, describing the district auditor's report as a 'devastating example of financial corruption and the abuse of power by senior members of the Conservative Party'. Jack Straw, Labour's environment spokesperson, added: 'This exposes political corruption on a scale unknown in post-war Britain. It is the stuff of banana republics. Responsibility for this goes right to the top of the Tory Party, which lauded and applauded Shirley Porter and her colleagues in 1990 and ever since.'

In response, Prime Minister John Major repeatedly refused to condemn the Council and told the House of Commons: 'We should wait and see precisely what the outcome might be. Otherwise we are in danger of assuming people have committed malpractice until they are proved innocent, which is no way to pass judgement.' Former Conservative Prime Minister Sir Edward Heath, however, had no such reservations. He said that, if true, the Westminster allegations were 'the heaviest blow the Conservative Party has had to take in living memory' (*Sunday Mirror*, 16 January 1994).

Following the publication of Magill's report, more revelations surfaced. On 16 January, the *Independent on Sunday* revealed the experience of Mark Green, a medical researcher, who paid £45,000 for a flat on the fifteenth floor of a block on the Warwick estate, on the Harrow Road, in 1989. The flat was subsequently valued at £62,000, but by 1994 estate agents had told him that his home was effectively worthless. As Mr Green explained: 'I and many others would have been happy to rent a council flat. But as they were all being sold off we would never have been able to rent in a million years.' He was assured that the whole estate had been designated for sale and that he would soon find himself surrounded by owner–occupiers rather than problem families. However, within weeks of moving in, Westminster was forced to drop its plans to sell more flats in the block following the furore created by *Panorama*. It was only three years later, when a neighbour tried to move, that owner–occupiers such as Mr Green discovered that estate agents and building societies would have nothing to do with the Warwick estate properties.

The other side of the Westminster tragedy was recounted by Maxine Sandford, who was born and brought up in the area. Together with her two young children she was rehoused to a leased flat in the East End, an hour from Westminster. Her unhappiness was clear: 'They moved me away from my family and friends without any regard for my, or my children's, health and happiness. It's miles from anywhere and very hard for anyone to visit me. It's become a nightmare; I want to be moved back to Westminster.'

Unsurprisingly, following the barrage of newspaper headlines, the Council suspended its designated sales policy on 18 January 1994, while at the same time claiming it was widely popular with residents. To reinforce the point, the Conservatives engineered a glowing letter of support from a group of grateful residents in Maida Vale, claiming that designated sales 'helped to keep families together'. Simon Milton said he was 'not at all surprised' by the group's letter: 'We have been inundated by calls from residents who are anxious for the scheme to continue. In all the furore over the district auditor's report the voice of Westminster residents has been drowned out. Over the years we have received thirty-eight petitions from residents to have their blocks designated and the policy of designated sales is as popular as ever.' Milton also claimed that, instead of costing the ratepayers £21 million, it had brought in £25 million for the Council.

Despite Milton's claims, the auditor was taking no chances. On 2 March he visited City Hall to take into joint custody further documents, after agreeing with the acting managing director, Bill Roots, that 'it would be prudent to place in their joint custody papers which may be relevant to these matters'. Magill, accompanied by four colleagues, collected thousands of pages of documents from a number of offices at City Hall, which were then placed in a locked room, with the keys held by himself and Roots.

On 26 January, a former vice-chairman of the Housing Committee, Michael Dutt, committed suicide and was found dead in his flat in St Albans with gunshot wounds. Dutt was one of those identified by Magill in his provisional report the previous week. Before his death he sent an open letter to Magill, via the *Evening Standard*:

Dear Mr Magill,
Your decision is both false and perverse, at least as far as I am concerned. It is untrue that I was aware of any kind of substantive policy to target the 'marginal' wards for political purposes.

I have, however, no confidence in your fairness or justice. Although I believe the High Court would reverse your finding, this together with hearing in the Appeal and House of Lords would last several years and consume resources and energy I do not have, while attempting to conduct my medical work.

I will not, therefore, propose to make further representations to you but please ensure this letter is read in full at any public hearing.
Yours sincerely,
M. Dutt

I first heard the news when I was called by Steve Boggan of the *Independent*, and was shocked that Dutt had been driven to take his own life. The Conservative response was predictable. Milton argued:

> We have to question a system of local government inspection which can allow the production of the most damaging report in the most lurid language before it has gone to court and then claim it is only a 'provisional' report, allowing it be widely repeated by the media. We also have to question a system that can allow loyal, hard working public servants to live with the threat of being professionally and financially ruined by enormous surcharges. (*Independent*, 28 January 1994).

This was followed a few days later, on 30 January, by an article by Stuart Greenman, Shirley Porter's assistant, in the *Mail on Sunday*. Greenman wrote:

> In the wake of his horrifying death, it's worth telling for the first time how that inquiry was conducted – its unfairness, the bullying, the almost Kafkaesque nightmare into which Dutt and others were sucked. At most interviews Magill, a thin, gaunt man with narrow-rimmed spectacles, was accompanied by a solicitor – the former legal adviser to Labour-run Greenwich – and two assistants. Together they crowded around Michael Dutt. Four against one.

Greenman's article had Roger Rosewell's fingerprints all over it. Rosewell was a key member of Porter's political machine. A man with an interesting political background, he was involved in her every move and, even today, acts as her spokesman. He helped her rise at Westminster and was a constant presence by her side throughout the birth of 'Homes for Votes' and the auditor's investigations. However, until the end of 1973 Rosewell was a senior member of the International Socialists, the neo-Trotskyist organisation which later became the Socialist Workers Party. Rosewell rose to the position of industrial organiser, responsible for encouraging workers' resistance to employers.

According to Patricia Kirwan, Rosewell became a regular presence in Porter's suite on the eighteenth floor of City Hall, interviewing officers and commenting on the content of reports and the progress of events. 'Staff are forbidden to mention his name and commonly refer to him in the Council corridors as "Thing",' she claimed. According to City Hall legend, when Rosewell visited Porter's office he used the goods lift at the back of the building. At some meetings, it was said, he would sit quietly at the back, jotting in his notepad. Often, some of those present had no idea who he was. Apparently, 'Thing' was also known as 'The Man with No Name'.

Rosewell, no doubt, also had a hand in Porter's mid-February letter to her 'thousands' of supporters and former colleagues in which she defended her position and promised to continue her fight:

> I will be returning to the UK to battle – to the European Court if necessary – to clear both my name and the reputation of Westminster City Council . . . To read some newspaper accounts one could be forgiven for thinking that I and others had been found conclusively guilty of wasting millions of pounds of council taxpayers' money by selling low cost homes to win an election . . . Nothing could be further from the truth.

But, far from returning to clear her name, on 26 March 1994 Porter and her husband left England to settle permanently in Israel.

With the City Council elections due just six weeks later, one might have expected that all the negative publicity about the Conservatives' gerrymandering activity would help Labour win back some of the seats lost four years earlier. Indeed, Labour

councillors piled on the pressure by compiling a hard-hitting
report on further 'Homes for Votes' allegations, this time claiming
that developers were required to build homes for sale, rather than
rented housing for the homeless and those on the housing waiting
list, as a condition of approval of planning consent.

But Labour's hopes of an election comeback were not looking
good, as a pre-election article on Maida Vale residents' views in
the *Independent* graphically illustrated on 13 April:

> We had a meeting and we were asked: 'Do you want these flats
> allocated to homeless people or do you want them to be put up for
> sale?' We had a vote and we voted for them to be designated for sale.
> The next day a letter arrived from Labour saying we were depriving
> homeless people of homes. But if you have a democratic vote, you
> must accept it. Putting the homeless in the flat two doors away made
> my life hell. Now there is a nice couple in there.

Labour might have also expected to benefit from a second
Panorama programme written by John Ware, who had presented
the original 1989 *Panorama* which sparked off the district auditor's
inquiry. This new *Panorama* was pulled from the schedules by
senior BBC management just ten days ahead of polling day.
Despite the strength of the Conservative majority at City Hall,
Conservative Central Office was very aware of the damaging
impact that more sleazy Westminster City Council stories would
have on the party's national image. Its pressure on the BBC
certainly worked.

On 5 May the Conservatives won the 1994 City Council
elections with the same thirty-seat margin as in 1990, winning
forty-five of the sixty seats. Once again I ran – and lost – in the
Cavendish ward, this time alongside Linda Hardman and David
Pitt-Watson. Eleven days after the elections, on 16 May 1994, the
BBC broadcast the second *Panorama* programme, again to critical
acclaim.

Following these further revelations, more objections to the
City Council accounts were submitted to the district auditor. This
time the objections were about the dirty tricks campaign against
Walterton and Elgin Community Homes (WECH), abuses of the

Council's planning powers, the misuse of Council resources in producing the Council newspaper *Ratepayer Reporter*, and housing homeless families in asbestos-ridden flats. The programme also revealed Porter's paranoia about her plans leaking to the Labour opposition. Her office at City Hall was swept for bugs every week.

Andrew Arden QC, in a legal opinion prepared for the Westminster Objectors, told *Panorama*:

> Nothing prepared me for such a naked abuse of power . . . They [the issues at the heart of the matter] are about values and conduct. They are about what is meant by local government professionalism. They are about what goes on behind closed doors, and how the money raised by local taxation is spent. They are about authority, and its use or abuse – members over officers, officers over one another . . . the corruption of the machinery of the authority as a whole.

The *Panorama* programme also revealed that the Council had lobbied the Housing Corporation not to provide funds for WECH's planned purchase of the Walterton and Elgin estates. But the Conservatives' victory in the 1994 Council elections did not stop John Magill's dogged and determined investigations.

11

The district auditor's public hearings

Mr Magill devoted one thousand hours or more annually for three or four years to the assignment. 'Frankly, it was never out of my mind. I went to bed thinking about it. I woke up in the middle of the night thinking about it. I woke up in the morning thinking about it.' His wife recently asked him whether he would be 'coming back to the family' after eight years.

Interview with John Magill, *Times*, 18 March 1998

John Magill, the district auditor, began his public hearings in the Council House, Marylebone Road, on 19 October 1994. They lasted thirty-two days and covered a period until 7 February 1995, and the Westminster Objectors raised almost £200,000 to pay for legal representation. The donations came in from across the country, mostly in small £5 and £10 amounts. At one point, the Post Office had to arrange a special delivery to the Objectors' treasurer, Steve Hilditch, so overwhelming was the public response to the appeal for funds.

Before the start of the hearings Shirley Porter and her colleagues waged an unsuccessful attempt to get the process further delayed so that Magill could be disqualified and replaced. Neale Coleman summed up the Objectors' frustration at Porter's never-ending attempts to use her wealth to wriggle from the district auditor's clutches with a defiant response: 'If you hurl enough lawyers at a thing like this you can hold it up for a year. But we won't give up, and the gerrymanderers should have got that message by now. If they have a logical explanation they should just give it.'

Westminster Tories were hopelessly split, with the deputy leader, Simon Milton, claiming: 'The Council has never been engaged in a policy of social engineering for political purposes. That is not what the Council is there for. The Council has not done that. None of the statistics, none of the facts, support that' (*Independent*, 13 October 1994).

Tony Prendergast, however, directly contradicted Milton on the BBC's *First Sight* programme. He said that councillors were misled over the findings of a report which found that Westminster was losing population: 'I think they decided to reinterpret some of the conclusions to suit their own means . . . trying to obtain a population which is more likely to vote Conservative than Labour.'

Patricia Kirwan told the auditor that her opposition to designated sales had eventually

> resulted in me being treated like a leftie. The reason I stood up against Dame Shirley was because I did not like her style. I didn't like her attitude and I didn't like her way of working. Officers were being bullied into doing work which was political because they were frightened of their jobs.

When the hearings did finally begin the revelations poured out at regular intervals. Early on it was revealed that Porter and her Conservative chairmen had agreed to monitor material likely to be made public at committee meetings. They were concerned that some of the things they planned to do should be kept private. In one memorandum, Porter told her colleagues: 'Loopholes have to be plugged to stop matters getting into the public domain.' This was followed by the former deputy City Solicitor Robert Lewis telling Magill that 'key wards' had crept into common parlance in the council as 'a love that dare not speak its name'. Lewis told the district auditor that it was clear to everyone that Council officers were doing some work of a party political nature. 'One could not simply go to the members and say, "We are going to stop all this", because we would all have been sacked; it was that kind of place.' Lewis described the Council in the late 1980s as 'a ruthless and highly politicised place'.

Meanwhile, Peter Hartley, the former Housing chairman, had a different view of Porter. He told the hearings that she 'was probably the most powerful person I have ever met' and 'kept control with mad hat schemes'. He said that when he heard of Building Stable Communities, he thought: 'Oh, my God, here we go again. This is this year's theme.'

The hearings revealed that seventy-two hostels had been identified in the eight key wards with a view to closing them down and selling them for conversion into smart flats that only the wealthy (who were assumed to be Conservative voters) could afford. A special team of planners and solicitors was proposed to hurry the process along and private investigators were employed to ferret out pretexts for shutting the hostels down.

The impact on individual Westminster families who were forced out of the area as a result of the designated sales policy was graphically described by the *Evening Standard*, which spoke to a number of young mothers who had accepted new flats in Hillingdon, ten miles away in outer London. Barbara O'Keefe, 29, was one of these. She was living in a one-bedroom flat in Pimlico with her two sons when Council housing officers told her that if she wanted a bigger home she would have to move to Hillingdon:

> I have lived in Westminster all my life. I like it, there was a real community spirit there. Moving here means I have to leave behind my mother, sister and all my friends. But what could I do? There were three of us in one small bedroom; I had to move to do the best by my kids.

Tara Simmonds, 25, used to live in Westminster with her baby son and was very bitter about the 'marginalisation' of single mothers: 'Why have we been shunted out here? It is as though we're not fit to be seen, as though we have nothing to offer' (*Evening Standard*, 1 November 1994).

As the hearings drew to a close another unexpected bombshell exploded when it was revealed that thousands of those who had bought flats from the Council had been given unlimited free repairs to their homes for life. This financial windfall to lessees, estimated to cost council tax payers nearly £30 million, was set out in a confidential 316-page report by the Council's internal auditors. The confidential report, which had been kept secret for at least a year, revealed that 6,700 people who bought homes from the Council since the mid-1980s had free or cheap service charges or had been given an indemnity against repair bills, some of which amounted to £20,000 per flat.

The report also revealed that many people facing service charges were not billed by the Council. This was done on Hartley's instructions after he received a memorandum from Graham England, director of Housing, which warned of 'substantial capital costs to be met by our lessees'. England told Hartley:

> Our whole home ownership policy, both right to buy and [designated] sales, could be affected by adverse publicity that this will generate and this could effectively deter purchasers. We must find a solution to this problem urgently. It may be possible by exploiting loopholes in the present regulations to avoid collecting charges from lessees.

After consulting lawyers, the Council went ahead with three schemes to help out lessees. The confidential report claimed that the legal advice appeared to have been misrepresented so that the Council could go ahead, and said that Hartley issued instructions that no major works bills should be issued to lessees. Anthony Scrivener QC advised the Council that a ten-year waiver from repair costs should only be allowed in exceptional cases. But the Conservatives decided to offer a ten-year waiver for all home-owners whose properties were on the listed works schedule. Scrivener also suggested that home-buyers should foot at least two-thirds of the bill for structural repairs. But, again, this advice was not included in the report to the committee. And although Scrivener's opinion only related to right-to-buy leaseholders, it was also used to justify policy for other house sales.

The result of this decision was that not one single bill was issued to lessees for four years, between 1987 and 1991. The £30 million cost of the schemes was borne by the Council's housing revenue account, which meant higher rents for Council tenants. Typically, instead of explaining the Council's extraordinary largesse to its

lessees, Bill Roots, the chief executive, huffed and puffed about
how the damning report found its way into the public domain: 'A
confidential internal audit report has been leaked to the media.
This action constitutes a serious breach of confidentiality which
the city council cannot ignore. I am considering whether to take
further action on this matter' (*Independent*, 1 February 1995).

The leaking of politically embarrassing confidential information
was of major concern to Westminster Conservatives. So much so
that, in October 1996, the Council proposed to the Nolan
Committee on Standards in Public Life that it should recommend
making it a criminal offence for councillors, officials and
journalists to leak confidential documents, even if it led to
exposing Council corruption.

The Council's submission, supported only by Conservative
councillors, claimed:

> At Westminster the disclosure of confidential documents has been a
> major problem . . . The media will encourage such leaks in the
> interests of exciting headlines . . . The release of confidential
> information, whether by members or officers, is rarely undertaken in
> the interests of local taxpayers but usually either for political or
> personal purposes. There is no straightforward answer but the
> proposals, which would make a deliberate breach of the new code of
> governance a criminal offence, would represent a major improvement
> on the situation.

And it was no surprise to learn, in January 1997, that the Council
had been unable to find out who was responsible for the huge
multi-million loss to the Council by not sending out bills to
lessees. Another confidential report concluded that the financial
losses were caused by monumental incompetence, rather than
political interference. Ratepayers would be excused if, at this
point, they were torn between laughing and crying at the goings-
on at City Hall.

At the close of the auditor's 32-day public hearings, despite all
the revelations, the Conservatives continued their 'we did
nothing wrong' line. Simon Milton argued: 'If we ensure all our
decisions are approved legally, yet an unelected arbiter can come

along years later and surcharge or disqualify us, then there is something very wrong with our system of democracy.'

The Council leader, Miles Young, went even further. He claimed that the district auditor's unfinished inquiry was seriously impeding councils' ability to take important decisions and deterring people from coming forward to serve as councillors. And in a final act of desperation the Conservatives wheeled out Lord Hailsham, the former Lord Chancellor, who was reported in the *Times* as saying: 'It is intolerable that this inquiry has taken so long.'

12

The district auditor's report

Magill's report is a devastating account of the wholesale subversion of a council's operations to further the interests of the ruling party. This was done at the expense of the borough's homeless people, whose interests were ruthlessly disregarded. But the Westminster scandal was not just about politicians behaving badly. The workings of the apolitical council bureaucracy were suborned. It was the permeability between party politics and council business that corrupted the democratic process.

The Prime Minister's refusal to utter a word of condemnation of this scandal is odious. His excuse that the legal process is not concluded is spurious. Regardless of any further legal proceedings, the evidence against these councillors and officers is damning. They had ample opportunity to defend themselves, but their defence was patent eyewash. If they continue now in office after all this, public cynicism about the democratic process will plumb still greater depths.

Melanie Phillips, *Observer*, 12 May 1996

Fifteen months after the public hearings, on 9 May 1996, John Magill issued his report on Designated Sales. His verdict was clear and unambiguous: 'I find as a fact that the Council was engaged in gerrymandering, which I have found is a disgraceful and improper purpose and not a purpose for which a local authority may act.'

Magill's report was devastating in the way that, one by one, he ripped apart the defences of the Conservative councillors and senior officers responsible. He found that the former Conservative chief whip Barry Legg

knew that it was wrong for the council to exercise its powers in order to secure an increase in the number of likely Conservative voters in marginal wards . . . In such circumstances a member has a duty to speak up. The evidence given to me by Mr Legg was that he was often absent from, or only attended parts of, meetings and that he was particularly engaged with his activities outside the council. He told me that he did not recall any discussion of targeting marginal wards. In my view, Councillor Legg was less than candid when he gave this evidence to me in interview. I find as a fact that he was aware . . . that Councillor Lady Porter proposed to give top priority to electoral success in evolving council policy on matters such as gentrification and homelessness.

Bill Phillips's 1988–9 correspondence with me came back to haunt him when Magill found that

Mr Phillips drafted his letter of March 22nd 1988 to Councillor Dimoldenberg so as to be economical with the truth and deliberately misleading. Mr Phillips knew that he and other officers (and members) were monitoring what was happening in key wards as Councillor Dimoldenberg had suggested but sought to obfuscate and deceive Councillor Dimoldenberg in order to hide the true position.

Magill also found that the Council's former director of Planning, Sydney Sporle, was aware of the party electoral reasons for the sale of council homes and criticised him for not speaking up. Paul Hayler, a senior housing officer, was found by Magill to have been 'recklessly indifferent' to the gerrymandering. And Matthew Ives, the City Solicitor, was the subject of pointed criticism: 'The case which the Objectors make against Mr Ives is a powerful one. In my view his failure to respond to the BSC targets paper or to make further enquiries was a serious error of judgement falling short of wilful misconduct by reckless omission.'

Magill's report included a long list of ways in which his 'investigations were not assisted', including 'shredding of documents', 'the Council being unable to locate a number of its own documents', 'the disappearance of the working documents and papers', 'delay by the Council and by officers in locating and providing documents' and 'the provision of inaccurate and, in some cases, misleading information by the Council and by interviewees, for example, as to whether particular meetings took place and to the status and authorship of documents'.

Crucially, Magill also found that councillors had a duty to 'blow the whistle' if they believed that wrongdoing was taking place. In a very strong passage in his report, Magill argued:

> In my view, a local authority Member is under a duty, so far as he/she reasonably can, to ensure that the local authority complies with the law and does not act unlawfully and that such a duty may require a Member to disclose the misconduct or suspected misconduct of other Members or officers of which he/she becomes aware. In such circumstances a Member has a duty to 'speak up' and do what else he/she reasonably can to protect the authority and the public from such misconduct and any consequences it may have had or has had.

As expected, Magill's report created a national storm. In Parliament Tony Blair told John Major that if he refused to condemn Westminster City Council, 'will it not be crystal clear to the British people that there are no depths to which the Conservative Party will not stoop to gain re-election to any office that it holds?' Immediately on the defensive, Major pledged 'to condemn cases of proven malpractice and those who have been found guilty in a court of law'. John Gummer MP, the then Secretary of State for the Environment, joined his leader and told the House of Commons: 'I have made it clear that I would condemn utterly any failure to meet the highest standards of propriety, whenever it is found and whoever is found guilty. If the decisions in respect of Westminster are upheld by the courts, I shall not hesitate to condemn those responsible.'

Despite their promises, neither Major nor Gummer has yet condemned Shirley Porter or the Westminster Conservatives for their illegal actions. Major's successors, William Hague, Iain Duncan Smith, Michael Howard and David Cameron, have all been similarly silent.

As expected, Porter, David Weeks and the others found by Magill to have been guilty of 'wilful misconduct' appealed to the High Court. The Conservatives also continued to try to undermine the district auditor's inquiry by criticising the cost and length of time it had taken and continuing their smear attack on Magill. Over the six-year period of his inquiry, the Conservatives made repeated attempts to disqualify him. Porter's lawyers consistently challenged his competence and impartiality. There were even suggestions that Magill was keeping himself in a job by prolonging the investigation.

Some years earlier, Porter had attacked Labour councillor David Pitt-Watson, who was at the time a partner with Touche Ross. Although Pitt-Watson had no financial relationship with Magill, she wrote to his firm suggesting that Pitt-Watson should step down from his job. She also organised an investigation by the Council, which showed that Pitt-Watson had acted entirely properly. But now the same smears were to be regurgitated, this time aimed at Magill. It came to a head during a House of Commons debate initiated by Labour on 14 May 1996. During the debate, the Conservative MP for Dover, David Shaw, a former business associate of Porter's son John, launched a series of allegations against those who had made the complaints to the district auditor. Typical of Shaw's attack was the following tirade:

> The district auditor's company, Touche Ross, has a connected company, Braxton Associates. One of its employees is a former Labour Westminster councillor, Mr David Pitt-Watson. He is a close political friend of the main objector, Mr Neale Coleman. So the district auditor's connected individual, who works in the group of companies that the district auditor is involved in, is a friend of the main objector. The district auditor's conflict in this instance is that the more Mr Pitt-Watson's friend, Mr Neale Coleman, objects to the accounts, the more Mr Pitt-Watson's employing partnership profits through more work for the district auditor . . . As one chartered accountant to another, I must tell Mr Magill that he has an impossible and appalling conflict of interest.

These were desperate times for the Conservatives and they were prepared to throw everything and anything they could get hold of to try to discredit Magill or their Labour tormentors.

13

Where was Porter's money?

Dame Shirley Porter has moved millions of Tesco shares from her own account into an undisclosed fund. Most of the shares were moved in 1994 after the district auditor, John Magill, issued his interim report. In the same year, Porter sold her penthouse flat near Hyde Park to her son. Inquiries by the *Sunday Times* suggest that if the courts find against Porter, Westminster council officials face a long hunt through a complex web of private trusts and offshore companies before they can recover the money. Porter and her husband have a history of using offshore funds to shelter the family's assets. In the early 1990s they used a Guernsey-based share account to shelter half the family's Tesco shares from capital gains.

According to a confidential section of the Tesco share register, Porter held 4.8 million shares in the company in 1990. This figure was reduced to 3 million in 1994, after which her shareholding was dismantled. Porter made three private share transfers in 1994, according to the register. Porter closed her holding with the final non-market transfer of 150,487 shares on October 24th 1994.

Sunday Times, 12 May 1996

John Magill's report found that the actions of Shirley Porter and her colleagues resulted in a loss to the Council of over £26 million, for which they were 'jointly and severally' responsible. As she had a reputed wealth of over £60 million, Porter was clearly able to pay all the money that was owing to the Council. She and her advisers knew this, and in 1994 they started to make the necessary arrangements to protect her wealth by moving it out of the UK.

Bizarrely, it was Westminster City Council which had the responsibility for collecting the £26 million surcharge from Porter and company. So, the Council, which had for years stead-fastly claimed that nothing wrong had taken place, was now responsible for collecting the biggest surcharge of all time. Not surprisingly, there were doubts as to whether the Conservative-run Council was going to take the task seriously or whether they would simply go through the motions.

Despite the district auditor's provisional report in 1994, it was not until 26 June 1996 that the Council appointed specialist forensic lawyers Stephenson Harwood to advise on how it should go about its responsibilities. A fortnight later, on 8 July, the Council's Policy and Resources Committee received confidential advice on 'whether some protective court proceedings should be taken to preserve [Porter's] assets'. The advice, from Stephenson Harwood and David Donaldson QC, was summarised in the report and stressed the difficulties and the complications involved.

Initially, the accountants KPMG were instructed to trawl through the records to find out where Porter's money might be. On 10 February 1997, John Fordham, a senior partner at Stephenson Harwood, wrote to the City Solicitor, Colin Wilson, to update him on KPMG's enquiries 'and I have reported orally on what has been learnt from them'. Surprisingly, nothing appears to have been put in writing by Stephenson Harwood or the Council about KPMG's findings. Interestingly, the fact that KPMG were commissioned by the Council was never reported to any committee at the time. It is possible that the chief executive, Bill Roots, did not put anything in writing because he believed that some Conservative councillors who had remained close to Porter might inform her of the Council's actions.

But if the Council was relaxed about chasing the Porter money, Labour councillors were certainly not. On 24 September 1997, the Labour Group leader, Alan Lazarus (who had succeeded Andrew Dismore following Dismore's election as MP for Hendon at the general election in May), sent a note to his Labour Group colleagues following a meeting with Roots two days earlier. Lazarus reported:

Roots has taken no further action to chase Porter's money, aside from the KPMG investigation. He says forensic accountants are very expensive and he has already exceeded his authority (financial or otherwise) in going so far. If WCC has to collect the money (i.e. when guilty) he will try to get a results-based contract.

On 16 October 1997 I was re-elected to the Council for the Queen's Park ward at a by-election following the election to Parliament of Karen Buck. There were many reasons why I put myself forward for the Queen's Park by-election. I still had much unfinished business at Westminster, not least the Porter affair. I also wanted to get back into active politics. I had been involved in Westminster politics since the late 1970s, and most of my friends were involved too. However, the main reason for wanting to get involved again was the election of a Labour government and the opportunity to make a difference at the local level.

I wanted to get involved with schools, too, now that Linda and I had two daughters, Amelia and Zoe, who were born in January 1994 and August 1995 respectively. I thought that, having a personal interest in improving local schools, I could inject a bit of passion into discussions. So, following the by-election, I went onto the Education Committee. However, before I could get down to work, Porter's High Court appeal decision intervened.

Just before Christmas, on 19 December 1997, Porter lost her High Court appeal. Three High Court judges, Lord Justice Rose, Mr Justice Latham and Mr Justice Keene, concluded:

> In our judgment, Dame Shirley Porter and David Weeks lied to us, as they had done to the auditor, because they had the ulterior motive of altering the electorate which they knew rendered targeting sales in marginal wards unlawful. Their purpose throughout was to achieve unlawful electoral advantage. Knowledge of the unlawfulness and such deliberate dressing-up both inevitably point to – and we find – wilful conduct on behalf of each of them.

Their Lordships ripped apart Porter's evidence:

> We reject that part of her affidavit which claimed that not all eight

wards were marginal: they were. She failed to explain to us why and by whom the eight wards were identified. In our judgment, this failure is explicable not by the effect of the subsequent passage of time on recollection, but by the realisation on her part that the more knowledge of detail which she admitted the more closely she would become identified with a policy of targeting designated sales to enhance Conservative prospects in marginal wards which she knew and knows now was unlawful.

Even those who were cleared of 'wilful misconduct', Peter Hartley, Graham England and Bill Phillips, were the subject of direct criticism. Hartley, according to the High Court,

> knew that the genesis and development of the policy to extend designated sales lay in the lead members' desire to add to the number of Conservative voters in marginal wards. We have no doubt that he knew that this was an improper purpose. He knew that in supporting the policy he would enable that improper purpose to be achieved. In doing so he was guilty of misconduct in that he was promoting a policy which was infected by that improper purpose.

Phillips's vital role in the process was clear. The High Court concluded: 'Phillips is an intelligent man who, no doubt, appreciates the unsatisfactory nature of the answers he has given . . . We take the view that he knew that what was proposed would give effect to an improper purpose and was therefore guilty of misconduct.'

And England, the High Court decided, knew exactly what was going on:

> We do not believe he was in any doubt that these were marginal wards chosen simply because of the perceived electoral advantage that designated sales would bring to the Conservatives in those wards . . . In our view, England must have appreciated that he was assisting the majority party to pursue its policy of seeking to obtain electoral advantage in the marginal wards . . . We take the view that he knew that it was inappropriate at the time . . . This does not mean, however, that he was guilty of wilful misconduct.

With such a devastating indictment of the actions of Porter and her colleagues, together with some of the most senior Council officers, one might have expected a degree of humility and remorse from the Conservatives, as well as an immediate concern to claw back the £26 million surcharge. But that was not to be. Right from the start the Council began to trot out all the reasons why it could not act to get back the money owed by Porter.

Within hours of the High Court decision, Roots issued a statement:

> We have received the High Court judgment and, until we have thoroughly examined it, we will not be in a position to respond. However, until the full appeals process is exhausted, the Council will not be in a position to begin proceedings to recover any money. If and when it becomes appropriate to begin such proceedings the Council will, of course, take the necessary action.

Roots's statement immediately fuelled suspicions that the Council would do just the bare minimum to recover the money.

At a celebration dinner at a restaurant in Sussex Gardens on 19 December, Labour councillors and friends met to toast the three High Court judges. Knowing of the Council's reluctance to act, we drafted a motion calling for an extraordinary meeting of the Council to instruct the chief executive to take all possible steps to recover the surcharge. Indeed, our concerns were widely shared and by 14 January 1998, 121 Labour and Liberal Democrat MPs had signed an early day motion which condemned the Council's 'failure . . . to take any steps whatsoever to recover the £27 million owed to the people of Westminster'.

As Andrew Dismore told the House of Commons on 21 January, 'So far, no action has been taken to recover the money from Dame Shirley. The Council has not even sent her a bill.' Andrew also pointed out tellingly that at the time of Mr Magill's report, 'I suggested that the Council should apply to the courts to freeze Lady Porter's assets. This did not happen, and we know that Porter has transferred most of her money abroad.'

It was left to *Punch* magazine to look into the future with remarkable accuracy, and to speculate on the likely outcome of the surcharge recovery:

> With most of her assets safely shuffled away abroad, and faced with a bill for £27 million, Porter could easily declare herself bankrupt. But family pride runs deep. Therefore, the most likely scenario, if push comes to shove, is that a deal will be made, with Porter agreeing to pay only a portion of what she owes.
>
> (*Punch*, 17 January 1998)

14

Chasing Porter's money: the Council prepares to do a deal

Officials of the council she once led are holding out the possibility of a deal by which Dame Shirley could escape some of the surcharge. They told investigators of a BBC2 programme that the amount of the debt must be balanced by the cost of pursuing it. Council officials say any effort to get cash back from abroad would involve a long and expensive legal battle.

Daily Mail, 14 October 1998

Tracking down Shirley Porter's money was never going to be easy, but right from the start, Westminster Conservatives never missed an opportunity to miss an opportunity. For example, in January 1998, *Private Eye* raised the possibility of the Council going to court to apply for a 'mareva' (freezing) injunction before Porter had moved all her assets abroad and asked: 'Why did Westminster Council not apply for a mareva? Its answer, which it says stems from legal advice from City lawyers Stephenson Harwood, is that it was "not appropriate" to do so' (*Private Eye*, 23 January 1998).

Despite informed speculation that Porter had employed the services of specialist financial help to move her money out of the UK, no attempt appears to have been made to follow up this information to locate her vast personal fortune. On 31 January 1998, an article in *Punch* revealed:

Those at Westminster City Council in charge of the hapless task of tracing the assets of Dame Shirley Porter, their former leader . . . might want to talk to a few individuals with a greater knowledge than most about the Great Dame's web of financial interests. Their first port of call should be Peter Green, of Personal Financial Management, based in Tunbridge Wells. PFM is adviser to the Dame Shirley Porter 1970 Settlement, the Chelwood Settlement and the Sir Leslie and Dame Shirley Porter 1965 Settlement. For more information on the latter, Westminster's crack investigators might wish to call Bank Cantrade, in Zurich.

There is no evidence that the City Council followed up this lead or even made a phone call to Switzerland to start inquiries. Indeed, ten days later, on 9 February, the City Council's Policy and Resources Committee received a confidential report headed 'Designated Sales Appeals – Legal Issues' which repeated the very conservative legal advice given to the committee on 8 July 1996. The report concluded: 'No recovery action as such is possible at this stage and it is not recommended that any protective court proceedings, such as application for a mareva injunction, be pursued in view of the substantial obstacles and risks involved in such proceedings.'

The Council was determined to do no more than they could get away with and this was reflected in the limited budget that was allocated. The confidential report argued:

In considering future action a balance needs to be struck. Doing nothing could lead to a delay and criticism if and when formal debt recovery becomes appropriate. Equally spending unduly large sums of public money now, when no debt may ultimately be due, would not be sensible. In the light of the advice received it is intended using a specialist firm. The costs of this plus associated further legal advice would be controlled so as to not exceed £50,000.

Despite these setbacks, we were determined to press the case. The Council meeting we called for back in December was eventually held on 18 February, and Alan Lazarus presented a petition signed by more than a thousand people. As is usual, the petition was referred to the Policy and Resources Committee, which did not meet until 20 April and predictably decided 'to note the petition and agreed that no further action is necessary at this stage'.

Behind the scenes, there appeared to be some vague signs of life. After a meeting with Bill Roots on 16 April 1998, Lazarus reported that Roots 'has been employing enquiry agents to confirm assets position in UK and advising on how to proceed in the US and Israel – meeting in a fortnight to review progress'. KPMG had also prepared an enormous chart showing foreign and off-shore interests, taking in such places as Israel, California, Switzerland, Panama, Luxembourg, and many tax havens, as well as an array of well-known individuals who were known to be connected with Porter and her family.

Meanwhile, the Council was continuing to lose millions of pounds on the designated sales legacy. And the human cost was still mounting, too. As the *Estates Gazette* revealed on 2 May 1998:

> Westminster lessees are bracing themselves to pay millions of pounds for council work on their homes that was completed up to 10 years ago. The dispute centres on a 10 year backlog for major works and on the failure of the council to manage the 37 different lease types issued to over 7,000 owners of former council flats. Westminster now expects to write off £16 million in irrecoverable debt and lost income. But the bottom line in the dispute is not money. A 64–year-old diabetic woman received notice from the council telling her that the cost of major works to her block of flats would be £16,000 per resident. Two weeks later she took an insulin overdose.

And predictably, despite the scandals, the lost millions and the human misery suffered by those unfortunate to be on the receiving end of the Conservatives' 'Homes for Votes' policies, the Conservatives easily won the May Council elections. Indeed, the Conservatives did more than just win. On 7 May 1998, they actually increased their majority on the City Council by narrowly winning two of the three seats in the Millbank ward from Labour, giving the Conservatives forty-seven seats with Labour holding just thirteen.

The increased majority, however, did nothing to increase the Conservatives' willingness to track down Porter's assets. Once again, on 9 May 1998, *Punch* pointed the Council in the direction of Peter Green, Porter's financial adviser. Again, there is no evidence that the Council followed this matter up. Indeed, all the authorities seemed remarkably relaxed about Porter's situation.

It even appears that in June 1998 Porter and her husband were invited to a party held at the official residence of the British ambassador to Israel in the hills of Ramat Gan, a suburb of Tel Aviv, to celebrate the Queen's birthday. Porter appeared to be enjoying life to the full, with a no-expenses-spared lifestyle involving south Pacific and Mediterranean cruises costing a reported £150,000.

Porter's lavish way of life contrasted starkly with those left behind in unsellable Westminster flats. Brian Pottle bought his mother's council flat in a twenty-storey Paddington tower block in 1989 for £17,000, hoping to sell it a few years later to raise enough money to pay for a nursing home for her. Instead he was hit with a demand for £6,000. In addition, because of the condition of the block, no mortgage lenders would give mortgages, making the flats impossible to sell.

Porter tried every trick in the book to try and claw her way out of trouble. In preparing for her case to overturn the High Court decision, she appointed Lord Neill, chairman of the Committee on Standards in Public Life, to be her counsel. Not surprisingly, this caused a massive political outcry and, on 23 June 1998, four days after Neill's appointment became public, he was forced to stand down when the House of Commons Public Administration Committee asked him for an explanation of his dual role.

Having failed to get Neill as her brief, Porter then tried to woo Roots. On 21 July, Roots met Porter in his office at City Hall for an off-the-record conversation. The details of this meeting did not come to light until 15 October, when Roots appeared on an issue of the BBC2 programme *First Sight*, entitled 'Looking for Shirley'. On that programme he revealed that the meeting had taken place and that a deal was 'something that may be appropriate in the fullness of time. The Council has spent £3.5 million in auditors' and legal fees to get to the point we're at now and we're still in the courts.' And it appeared that Roots wasn't the only person from City Hall that Porter and her advisers were talking to at that time.

On 25 August 1998, the *Daily Express* ran a story about private eyes employed by the City Council who

> had found a UK asset overlooked by KPMG. This consisted of two pieces of land in the far north of Scotland, a total of more than 1,500 acres purchased in the early eighties by Dame Shirley in her own name. Before Westminster Council was able to act, Lady Porter suddenly sold both pieces of land in Scotland to a company called Oakum Association Ltd. That was on June 10, only a couple of weeks after Westminster's investigators had identified the asset. Westminster Council has refused to tell the *Express* who precisely was privy to this information and the strong suspicion must remain that someone at the Council leaked the information to Lady Porter, who promptly sold the land.

Later that day Alan Lazarus wrote an angry letter to Roots demanding a full inquiry. Roots's reply to Lazarus on 9 September revealed an even more bizarre situation. In denying that there had been a leak of information to Porter from either the Council or Stephenson Harwood, Roots claimed:

> The factual position is that the City Council, for reasons of confidentiality, has never had a copy of the private investigations report in its possession. Their work was directly commissioned by Stephenson Harwood solely to enable them to advise on an appropriate recovery strategy, should this be appropriate in due course. The City Solicitor believes that he recalls Stephenson Harwood mentioning that the investigators had identified an asset in the UK, but only in general terms, not in the detail set out in the press report.

Lazarus responded on 17 September to ask

> why it took a firm of private investigators to identify Porter's ownership of the forestry when this fact had been known to the Council since at least 1992. A simple search through the Council's records reveals Porter's reference to 'ownership and management of Scottish Woodlands' (note plural) in her Declaration of Interests of the

same year. It seems to me that the Council cannot see what is under its nose.

Despite Roots's pledge to mount an inquiry, there is no evidence that he did. There is certainly no evidence of a report to councillors on the Scottish woodlands leak. At the same time, Roots used *First Sight* and subsequent media interviews to lower expectations and to stress how difficult and expensive the recovery process had become. He told the local press: 'There is no debt for us to recover at this stage. If she is found to be innocent it is the end of the debt. I do not want to spend hoards of money on something that is speculative' (*Westminster and City Mail*, 16 October 1998). And to demonstrate the relatively small amount of money being invested by the Council in tracking down the Porter millions, a confidential report to the Policy and Resources Committee on 30 March 1999 revealed: 'The costs incurred to date since the previous report total approximately £43,000 which includes the fees of the investigators, foreign lawyers and Counsel. Some further expenditure will be required to complete the City Council's state of readiness in relation to possible proceedings, but these will not exceed £20,000.'

This reluctance to act was obviously another reason why the Council failed to follow up John Porter's involvement with his mother's finances, so clearly identified in *Punch* a year later. This article, 'Why Shirley's boy is the Porter who carries bags of money' by Pete Sawyer, could not have been clearer:

> It was John Porter who was instrumental in keeping Dame Shirley's fortune out of the hands of John Magill, Westminster's District Auditor. Faced with the prospect of his mother losing part of her personal fortune, John Porter has taken control of the majority of her British interests. Westminster Council, wary of the enormous cost of tracing Porter's assets overseas, and reluctant to pursue the case for political reasons, has more or less given up the chase. (*Punch*, 28 June 2000)

There is no evidence that the Council did anything to act on this information. Three years later, almost to the day, the full extent of

John Porter's involvement with his mother's finances was broadcast by the BBC and the net began to tighten around Shirley Porter's millions.

15

A council addicted to scandal

If an entire council leadership can be said to be in denial, then it is the Tory-run Westminster City Council, in relation to the biggest gerrymandering scandal in the modern history of local government. This time last year Dame Shirley Porter and her deputy David Weeks were found guilty in the High Court of 'wilful misconduct', gerrymandering and vote-rigging. . .

Ever since then, Westminster Council has been making efforts, open or covertly, to shift the retribution on to local taxpayers, not least by declining to take any action to recover the £28 million until the appeals process had been exhausted – a process which could take many more years. Its latest gambit is to recommend that those involved in the gerrymandering should be awarded compensation, if the latest appeal against the High Court ruling fails – despite legal advice that it has no obligation to compensate those involved, and that none of those who would get it have been totally exonerated, to put it charitably.

Evening Standard, leader, 15 December 1998

There was never a dull moment as a Westminster City councillor! At some points it seemed as if there was not a week that went by without another scandal hitting the news. It was as if the Conservatives couldn't help themselves. They were addicted to scandal and could not kick the habit. The autumn of 1998 was one of those times.

At the end of October the Council attempted to use the Local Government Boundary Commission to abolish the Church Street ward, one of Labour's safest wards, and one which had elected Labour councillors since before the Second World War. The Conservatives planned to abolish the ward and divide the 6,800 voters between three neighbouring wards. There was no justification for this whatsoever, other than for the Conservatives to gain a political advantage.

This was followed, on 30 November 1998, with the publication of a damning report by the local government ombudsman, Edward Osmotherley, into the way in which the owners of the cockroach-infested Clarendon Court Hotel in Maida Vale raked in £750,000 in housing benefit from the Council while accommodating homeless families in appalling conditions. The 79-page report revealed that the Council had first been informed of the problem in 1988 but took no effective action until 1995, and that it was only because Labour councillors took the story to the press that the Council was forced to act.

The ombudsman awarded £5,500 between six asylum-seekers and their families from Colombia, Sudan and Bosnia, who were forced to live in the squalid, overcrowded conditions in the Maida Vale hotel. Osmotherley said of one family's case:

> The carpets, curtains and blankets had been filthy when they started living there and they had to get them cleaned themselves. The room was infested with cockroaches twenty-four hours a day. Their second child was born in July 1995. Mrs B says she found cockroaches on the baby's lips and in her ears, and the baby had facial infections as a result. The Bs say it is not unusual for them to find cockroaches all over their own faces when they awake in the morning.

The owners were fined just £8,000 and later sold the hotel for luxury flats for millions of pounds. The then leader of the Council, Melvyn Caplan, brazenly claimed: 'We acted very quickly once we knew about the problems' (*Guardian*, 10 December 1998).

And just before Christmas it was revealed that the Council was about to pay legal bills totalling £700,000 for a number of Conservative councillors and Council officers involved in the 'Homes for Votes' district auditor investigations. This proposal, unsurprisingly, created a storm. The Council was forced to bow to the huge chorus of disapproval and hold fire on the decision to reimburse the legal costs of Conservative councillors Barry Legg,

Alex Segal and Miles Young, and Council officers Graham England, Sydney Sporle and Ken Hackney, all of whom were investigated by the district auditor but were subsequently found not guilty of wilful misconduct.

The Council had previously sought government permission for the payments, with an application to John Gummer, the former Environment Secretary, before the May 1997 election. Gummer, however, did nothing about it and left it for his successor, John Prescott. Not surprisingly, Prescott refused to sanction the payments. John Magill also took legal advice and refused the Council permission to pay out the cash. However, a new district auditor, Brian Willmore, who did not take legal advice, left it to Westminster to decide what it wanted to do.

In the end the Council decided that there was legal doubt about its ability to grant the money and it could not go ahead after Prescott had refused to sanction its spending the money. To clear the legal doubts, the Council encouraged the officers' trade union to take judicial review action in the High Court, which resulted in a green light to pay the legal costs. Eighteen months later, on 18 July 2000, the Council decided to do what it always wanted to do and agreed to pay up. Segal and Young received £79,738 plus interest. Legg received £216,705. In addition, England, Hackney, Sporle and another Council officer, Paul Hayler, received £481,153. No doubt with tears in his eyes, a Council spokesman later told the *West End Extra* on 20 July 2000: 'There was in reality very little choice but to agree reimbursement of the legal expenses claimed and the committee took the view that it would be inequitable not to also pay reasonable interest.'

Indeed, the Conservatives' capacity for 'forgiving and forgetting' and 'moving on' was neatly illustrated in January 1999 when Porter was invited to the Lord Mayor's reception at the five-star Landmark Hotel in Marylebone. Not so forgiving was the new district auditor, Derek Chilcott, whose confidential report on the Council's failure to charge lessees for repairs found its way into the hands of the *Guardian*. The Council's failures had cost council tax payers £12.5 million.

Westminster Conservatives and senior Council officers were angry that their embarrassing failures had been made so public. On

19 October 1999, *Guardian* journalist David Hencke revealed the way in which the Council dealt with people who had the nerve to criticise it publicly:

> Last week I was asked to go to Charing Cross police station to be questioned by Scotland Yard's organised crime squad for my heinous misconduct in writing an article revealing that a fresh district auditor's report was about to damn the former Conservative council leader Dame Shirley Porter. My alleged crime was that of 'aiding and abetting' an unknown leaker to reveal the findings of a confidential auditor's report condemning her activities without first getting the author's or Westminster council's permission. They wanted me to tell them my sources so – presumably – they could prosecute them and bang them in jail. I refused to cooperate.

A longer running scandal involved Dolphin Square, a complex of 1,200 apartments, for which the Council had acquired a long lease in 1964 when it rescued residents from the square's previous cash-strapped owner. Built in the mid-1930s, Dolphin Square was famous for housing members of Parliament, civil servants and a number of household names ranging from Princess Anne to Mandy Rice-Davies. The Council rescue deal was masterminded by the Westminster town clerk, Sir Alan Dawtry, who went on to live in one of the square's eighth-floor penthouses and chair the Dolphin Square Trust (DST), the organisation which ran the complex. From 1964 onwards Dawtry and his DST colleagues, who include a posse of former Lord Mayors of Westminster – including Tony Prendergast and Alan Bradley – and City Council chief officers such as David Hopkins and Rodney Brooke (who is the current DST Chairman), ran Dolphin Square like a colonial outpost of City Hall.

Despite Dolphin Square having the status of a housing association, in its forty-year life the trust did not house a single person from the Council's housing waiting list. Instead it operated a unique housing policy of subsidising rents from the surplus of running one of the blocks, Rodney House, as a hotel. As a result, long-standing Dolphin Square residents enjoyed the lowest social housing rents in London. For over thirty years, the Council turned a blind eye to this scandal, claiming it could do nothing about it.

Then, in the late 1990s, the Conservatives realised that they were sitting on a very valuable asset and promptly went looking for a buyer. Not surprisingly, the DST was not amused. And neither were residents, when the Council tried – after thirty-five years – to enforce a covenant in the trust's lease that gave the Council the power to approve rents. Of course, the Council had never previously tried to influence rents as it had been hand in glove with the trust's policy of running the square as a private fiefdom, immune from the responsibility of housing the homeless. But now the Council was threatening to put Dolphin Square rents up to the same level as Council rents in other parts of Pimlico – the highest in London.

Oblivious to the outcry from long-standing residents, many of whom were pensioners of modest means who had planned their lives on the basis that rents would stay low, the Conservatives sold Dolphin Square to US investors Westbrook in 2005 for over £200 million, half of which went into a housing charity. Almost at once long-time residents began to leave Dolphin Square as they were offered the choice of taking a new lease at a market rent or accepting money to leave. Most decided that life at Dolphin Square would never be the same and took the money.

16

Porter wins in the Court of Appeal – but the House of Lords tells her to pay up

If this is how the law stands then the law is an ass and should be changed. A councillor's first and only duty should be to his or her constituents and local community. Yesterday's judgment apparently gives councillors carte blanche to squander local taxpayers' money for party political gain. If the ruling is not overturned by the Lords then the Government must change the law.

Daily Express, 1 May 1999

The spring of 1999 brought Shirley Porter her only victory in the seventeen years of the 'Homes for Votes' saga. In March the Court of Appeal upheld her appeal on a 2:1 majority. Porter threw everything at the Court of Appeal to try and win her case, including invoking a recent case involving the Chilean dictator, General Augusto Pinochet, as well as arguing that Sir David Keene, one of the original High Court judges, should have been ruled out because he once lent his house in the south of France to Tony Blair.

At the start of the appeal Porter's counsel, the Liberal Democrat Lord Lester QC, told the hearing:

She has suffered stress and anxiety in the course of this lengthy and disproportionate investigation. The mud that was slung at Dame Shirley has undoubtedly stuck to her, and it has entirely marred her political and personal reputation across the country. Throughout the seven years of the investigation, her family and social life have been disrupted, she has incurred ever-mounting legal costs and has remained uncertain as to the outcome and the sanction.

Porter's victory by a 2:1 majority was on the grounds that politicians were entitled to make 'voter-pleasing decisions' to their party's advantage. One of those who agreed with Porter, Lord Justice Schiemann, concluded:

> Voter-pleasing decisions are lawful even if one of the motivating factors in the minds of councillors who vote for them is the desire to be re-elected. It is clear to me Dame Shirley was seeking to avoid doing anything illegal and that this was the reason why she laid bare her hopes to her legal advisers and asked for legal advice.

However, in his dissenting judgment, Lord Justice Walker made this telling point:

> The overall impression throughout, from mid-1986 to mid-1989, is that the most influential members of the Conservative group on the City Council, led by Dame Shirley Porter and Mr Weeks, had electoral advantage as the overriding objective in formulating their housing policy, securing its adoption by the Council, and implementing it with high priority given to marginal wards. The City Solicitor was correct when he wrote on the agenda for the working lunch on 3 August 1987: 'This paper shows officers working for a Tory victory.' The same comment could have been made about dozens of other similar papers produced at the expense of council tax payers in the City of Westminster. What occurred cannot realistically be described as officers providing factual information to elected members, nor simply as elected members allowing the occasional thought of possible electoral advantage to cross their minds.

Porter was triumphant. 'The sun shines on the righteous,' she told the *Sun* (1 May 1999) after her victory over 'the bunch of oddballs and guttersniping screwballs', as she fondly described her opponents (*Guardian Weekly*, 9 May 1999). A more common reaction was that summed up by Neale Coleman: 'It is astonishing if any council has the right to rig elections by using public funds to manipulate the electorate. If the Lords uphold this the government will be forced to change the law.'

This was the first real set-back in the ten-year campaign for justice. Thankfully, the district auditor was given leave to appeal to the House of Lords. However, the victory gave Porter and her colleagues the opportunity to try to occupy the moral high ground and criticise the district auditor for the costs of the inquiry in an attempt to persuade the Audit Commission not to pursue the House of Lords appeal.

Porter's supporters briefed the *Times* to run the story that council tax payers could face a bill of £10 million, while the *Local Government Chronicle* reported an Audit Commission spokesman saying:

> There are concerns about how much this has cost and how long it's taken. One former commissioner said: 'There will be a big argument for dropping the case within the commission. Every penny spent now will be lost whether or not Magill won an appeal because he will not recover any surcharge.' Most commentators are convinced Mr Magill will never recover a penny in surcharge. (*Local Government Chronicle*, 7 May 1999)

Porter herself tried for the sympathy vote in a *Sunday Telegraph* interview:

> The legal process is so expensive. The strain is unbelievable. But I come from a fighting family and I knew I had done no wrong. As far as I am concerned you come into this life with nothing but your good name. And I want to go out with mine. It's been 10 years since I have been allowed to talk. That is definitely the most frustrating experience of my life for someone who is used to talking to the press. I hope that the auditor will now realise that this case should go no further. Two senior judges have exonerated me and my colleagues. Of course I am thrilled, but I have mixed feelings about the whole process. I have had the financial and emotional means to fight but others have not been so fortunate. People have lost their lives and careers in this process. Any why? Because I wanted to run the best council in the country. (*Sunday Telegraph*, 2 May 1999)

The attacks on John Magill started up again in earnest. A nasty unsigned article in the *Local Government Chronicle* branded him as 'local government enemy no. 1', in an attempt to stop him appealing to the House of Lords. Porter then told *Accountancy Age*: 'His lawyers are arguing that unless they contest this judgment they will be liable to pay my costs, on top of the costs they have already paid out to other cleared defendants. Apparently they think it's worth risking another £1 million in the Lords to reverse this verdict' (*Accountancy Age*, 3 June 1999). Thankfully, the Audit Commission ignored Porter's advice and, on 17 June 1999, Magill confirmed that he was going ahead with the House of Lords appeal.

Porter's brief moment of success came to a sudden end on 13 December 2001 when the Law Lords unanimously upheld the High Court ruling and found Porter and David Weeks guilty of 'political corruption' and ordered them to pay up the £26 million surcharge. Their Lordships condemned 'the history of pretence, obfuscation and prevarication' that surrounded the policy, and the 'intensive camouflage' Porter and Weeks had used to hide their actions.

Lord Bingham came to a series of damning conclusions:

> The passage of time and the familiarity of the accusations made against them cannot and should not obscure the unpalatable truth that this was a deliberate, blatant and dishonest misuse of public power. It was a misuse of power by both of them, not for the purposes of financial gain but for that of electoral advantage. In that sense it was corrupt.
>
> The corruption was not money corruption. No one took a bribe. No one sought or received money for political favours. But there are other forms of corruption, often less easily detectable and therefore more insidious. Who can doubt that the selective use of municipal powers in order to obtain party political advantage represents political corruption? Political corruption, if unchecked, engenders cynicism about elections, about politicians and their motives, and damages the reputation of democratic government.

Bingham also highlighted the unacceptable behaviour of senior Council officers at the time. He continued: 'There were deliberate attempts by officers to conceal the system of monitoring which had been established by giving deliberately misleading answers to proper questions from members of the minority party on the Council.'

South African-born Lord Scott of Foscote, who as Sir Richard Scott produced the report into the 'Arms to Iraq' affair, vindicated our strategy of working closely with the BBC *Panorama* team to expose the evil at the heart of the Council. He observed:

> When detected and exposed it must be expected, or at least it must be hoped for, that political corruption will receive its just deserts at the polls. Detection and exposure is, however, often difficult and, where it happens, is usually attributable to determined efforts by political opponents or by investigative journalists or by both in tandem.

Porter, once again, reverted to her standard policy of denial and 'we did nothing wrong'. She told the *Daily Mail*:

> I am not corrupt. I did not abuse power. It is utterly unfair that I alone among all local authority leaders should be singled out and ordered to pay for promoting the right to buy. My faith in British justice has been shaken. I intend to fight this case in the European courts.
>
> (*Daily Mail*, 14 December 2001)

Porter's friends in the press followed on in her support. The former *Times* editor William Rees-Mogg, husband of Westminster Conservative councillor Gillian Rees-Mogg, argued that, following Magill's press conference in January 1994 where he announced his provisional findings, he should 'have agreed to stand down. Withdrawal at that point would have cost Mr Magill, or his practice, the loss of very substantial fees' (*Times*, 17 December 2001).

Taking a more balanced view, the Audit Commission solicitor, Rod Ainsworth, commented: 'The case was not just about lost taxpayers' money. It confirms standards of conduct of senior councillors, the appropriate use of public funds and the right of local people to challenge the behaviour of their councils.' In other words, the district audit system had worked. The issue was now about how to collect the money from Porter after she had been allowed by the Council to move her £60 million fortune out of the UK unheeded since she and her husband left for Israel in 1994, seven years previously.

The day after the Lords judgment, on 14 December 2001, the Council announced that its director of Legal Services, Colin Wilson, had used his delegated authority 'to institute proceedings, or take such other steps as may be necessary, to enforce any debt, or the benefit of any covenant or other obligation to the Council'. Six days later, on 20 December, the Council leader, Simon Milton, wrote to all staff to try and finally draw a veil over the dark Porter years – without mentioning her name:

> You will no doubt have seen the extensive press coverage of this long running court case. Now that the decision is final it brings an end to a matter that has dogged this authority for too long.
>
> However, I would remind you that this is as a result of decisions taken almost fifteen years ago and relates to circumstances that have long since changed.

Of course, Milton omitted to apologise for the huge financial loss to council tax payers and for the lives that had been ruined by the Council's unlawful 'Homes for Votes' policies. His ambivalence about collecting the surcharge, as well as his enduring sympathy for Porter, were beautifully illustrated in an interview he gave the local press on 21 December:

> The process has cost us £7 million and there is no certainty that we will be successful in our claim. I cannot estimate how much the legal proceedings may cost but it will be money that could be spent on services. The current housing shortage has nothing to do with Dame Shirley Porter. I feel sad for the individuals because they believed they were genuinely serving the public. (*Paddington Times*, 21 December 2001)

Six months previously, in June 2001, and prior to the Law Lords' decision, Milton and chief whip Robert Davis dined out with Porter and her husband at a Tel Aviv restaurant. They were accompanied by Councillors Angela Hooper (chairman of the Council's Standards Committee) and Ian Wilder, who were in Israel to attend the wedding of Wilder's daughter. When later challenged about the propriety, as Council leader, of meeting with Porter when it was very possible that the Council would later have the responsibility of collecting the largest ever surcharge in local government history, Milton merely shrugged it off.

17

The Council finally starts the 'hunt' for Porter's money

The Tesco heiress appears to have been most shrewdly advised on her finances at the height of the affair, in 1994. Within nine months, she had ensured a drastic change to most of her assets. At one stage she had owned 5.5 million shares in Tesco which were worth more than £10 million. After 1994, all references to her had disappeared from the company records, either because she had sold her shares or because they had been transferred to another name. According to the company's share register, Dame Shirley made three private share transfers in 1994, with the final move being made on 24 October. Other investments were moved into trusts in Panama and Guernsey. The Porters used a Guernsey-based share account to shelter their cash from capital gains in the early 1990s. Large chunks of the Porter fortune have undoubtedly been sunk into charitable works in Israel.

Independent, 3 January 2003

Initially the Council, with the spotlight firmly in its direction, moved into gear quickly. After all, it had had many years to prepare so there could have been no excuse for any delay. On 28 December 2001 the Council obtained a freezing order from the High Court against Shirley Porter's assets world-wide.

However, right from the start, we were suspicious of the Council's real intentions. At the Council meeting on 16 January 2002, in response to a request for an assurance that the Council would do everything it could to collect the money, Simon Milton replied: 'I can assure Councillor Lazarus that I, and the deputy leader, will be monitoring these matters closely and, in particular, monitoring the costs of recovery, which are also of importance to the residents and taxpayers of Westminster.' As before, the determining factor in how hard the Conservatives would try to recover the surcharge was the cost.

In response to the freezing order, on 9 January 2002 Porter disclosed in a sworn affidavit that she had assets of just £300,000 world-wide. The details of Porter's 'wealth' were leaked to the *Daily Mirror*, which reported on 28 January 2002 that she was 'down to my last few pounds'. The article summarised her newly lost wealth as £50 in a Coutts bank account; an £18,000 share in a London flat; a few hundred pounds in an offshore account in Jersey; a private company in the British Virgin Islands with a cash balance of £20,000; thirty items of paintings and furniture, plus books of prints and etchings and some jewellery; £300,000 worth of silver, paintings and sculptures owned with her husband, including a portrait of herself; and a one-fifth share of a yacht worth £4,000.

According to the Council's director of Legal Services, Colin Wilson, 'this article was based on confidential papers apparently removed from the court . . . This situation was investigated by the Police but the Attorney General has decided to take no action.'

Two days later, on 30 January, the *Mirror* reported that Porter and her husband had taken a sixteen-day cruise in the south Pacific on the six-star liner *Silver Wind*, occupying the Grand Suite at a cost of £90,000.

Porter was making the Council look even more foolish than everyone thought it was. By the end of March 2002 the Council had spent £100,000 on legal costs and had recovered nothing. Moreover, Porter was taking her fight to the European Court of Human Rights in Strasbourg in an attempt to overturn the House of Lords' decision. However, suspicions that the Council was simply 'going through the motions' were fuelled by a report in the *Evening Standard* in February: 'Privately, many councillors are thought to be pessimistic about the prospect of getting anything back. However, they feel obliged to be seen to be making an effort, if only to counter suggestions that the authority – which is still Tory-run – is being soft on its former leader.'

Not content with just sitting back and leaving it to the Conservatives to allow Porter's millions to slip away, Labour continued to press the Council. In late March 2002, Karen Buck MP wrote to the chief executive, Peter Rogers, to suggest that the Council should consider similar action to that taken in respect of Fouad al-Zayat, which had been reported in a recent edition of the *Sunday Times*, where, 'under an order in the High Court Queen's Bench Division earlier this month, Zayat was told he must surrender his passport if he returns to Britain. He will not be allowed to leave the country until he reveals the whereabouts of all his assets.' As ever, there is no evidence that the Council ever considered this option.

And, once again, there was no evidence that the 'Homes for Votes' scandal had any damaging impact on the Conservatives' local electoral fortunes. Indeed, at the elections on 2 May 2002 the Conservatives again increased their majority by winning forty-eight of the sixty seats on the Council, following boundary changes involving the splitting-up of the marginal Millbank ward and the creation of two new safe Conservative wards. Alan Lazarus had stood down from the Council on his move to east London. In his place, one of the youngest members of the Labour Group and a local GP, Simon Stockill, was elected leader of the group.

The elections brought no further progress on recovering Porter's money. In reality, the situation was actually getting worse. In a Commons debate, Peter Bradley MP revealed that on 14 May 2002 there were 'sales of Tesco shares to the value of £1.2 million, in which Shirley Porter had an interest, just a few months after she had disclosed assets of no more than £300,000' (Hansard, 30 June 2004). Further bad news was the Council's determination to stop John Magill publishing a public interest report on the further objections to designated sales, which he had been investigating since the mid 1990s.

On 12 July 2002, Rogers wrote to Magill's solicitors to try to stop publication of the public interest report on the grounds of cost. In his letter Rogers made a clear connection between the publication of the report and the doubtful prospects of recovering any money from Porter. He argued:

The City Council has already expended substantial sums in meeting the Appointed Auditor's fees in respect of the previous audit investigation and hearing into the designated sales matter (in excess of £3 million) and is currently spending substantial sums in seeking the recovery of the sum certified as due in respect of that matter, with no certainty of a successful outcome.

A week later, on 19 July, the Council's pessimistic approach to recovering the Porter surcharge was revealed in a confidential report to the Cabinet member for Finance, Kit Malthouse, from Colin Wilson, director of Legal and Administrative Services. The report discussed various legal points in relation to the arguments about the amount of interest owed by Porter (either £1.247 million or an amount in excess of £13 million) and concluded that the point was largely academic:

> Although the City Council might be successful in identifying further assets, or, possibly, setting aside transactions which have divested Dame Shirley Porter of assets, on the basis of what is currently known, any amount which ultimately proves recoverable is likely to fall well short of the principal sum of £26 million, let alone the gross figure of the principal sum plus interest.

Despite the Council's pessimism, on 30 July Porter was ordered by Lord Justice Hart to pay an increased surcharge of £39,960,000, in respect of her breach of trust. Meanwhile, by 1 August the Council had spent over £200,000 on legal and recovery costs since the House of Lords judgment.

Labour still kept on asking questions to keep the Conservatives focused on collecting the Porter loot. On 11 September, Murad Qureshi, Labour's finance spokesperson, raised the issue at a meeting of the Finance and Support Services Overview and Scrutiny Committee. As the minutes of the meeting clearly show, Qureshi was told to mind his own business: 'In answer to a query raised by Councillor Murad Qureshi about the collection of monies recoverable from Dame Shirley Porter, the Chief Executive advised that the Council were currently examining strategies to retrieve monies owed to the Council and investigations were ongoing and would remain confidential until further notice.' Qureshi's question, however, forced the Council to admit that it had still made no real progress in collecting the Porter surcharge. Council press officers suggested that declaring Porter bankrupt might be a possibility, but the low expectations that the Council was keen to encourage shone through the Council's prepared statement: 'The Council is committed to pursuing the debt vigorously, although bearing in mind the relatively limited value of assets disclosed, any substantial recovery of the surcharge is likely to depend on whether assets transferred by Dame Shirley in the past can be pursued.'

By the end of September 2002, despite running up a legal bill of £250,000, no money had yet been recovered. As a note of a meeting held on 27 September between the City Council, Stephenson Harwood, the district auditor and the Audit Commission reveals:

> Colin Wilson confirmed that the City Council . . . looked to be exhausting conventional measures that might be taken. On advice from Stephenson Harwood they propose to take further proceedings to attempt to widen the freezing/disclosure orders currently in place against Dame Shirley. John Fordham cautioned that there is no clear precedent for the court's willingness to grant such an extension. The purpose of their application specifically is to attempt to put pressure on Dame Shirley's known associate, Peter Green, through whom it is believed that she had arranged her affairs.

So, at last, the Council had got round to identifying Peter Green as a key player in the Porter money world. Of course, it had been tipped off about Green's pivotal role years ago but had done nothing about it.

It was not until 6 November that the Urgency Committee of the Cabinet met for the first time, in private, to discuss the Porter surcharge recovery – ten months after the House of Lords' judgment. The committee comprised just three Conservative councillors. By November the Council's legal bill had increased to £308,470 and Porter had still not paid a bean. The committee did not meet again until 18 August 2003 – nine and a half months later.

The November 2002 meeting agreed to apply to the High

Court to widen the freezing and disclosure order, obtained in December 2001 against Porter's assets world-wide, with a view to freezing her interests in previously transferred assets. This decision was made eleven months after Porter had made her initial incomplete disclosure. The Council has never given any reason for the eleven-month delay in seeking a wider freezing and disclosure order.

Whatever the reason for the delay, Porter's glittering lifestyle did not appear to be troubled. On 10 November 2002, just four days after the Council's decision to apply to extend the freezing order over her assets, she and her husband attended a dinner at the British embassy in Israel at the invitation of the British government. Later, following questions from Norman Baker MP to Mike O'Brien MP, a Foreign Office minister, about the dinner invitation, it would appear that Porter's £42 million debt for the biggest-ever scandal in local government history did not register on the Foreign Office radar.

Towards the close of 2002, the Council was getting increasingly desperate to show some return for twelve months' work and over £300,000 of legal costs. So it started to brief the press in order to show how difficult the job was and how it was still very much committed to collecting the money. The result was an article in the *Independent*: 'Shirley Porter has found sanctuary in Israel, but the bloodhounds of Westminster City Council are closing in'. The source for the article has never been revealed but it contains a massive amount of information about Porter's assets previously only included in the confidential report to the Urgency Committee of the Cabinet on 6 November. The article also contained details of the Council's future recovery strategy, which could have only have been revealed to the *Independent* by a Council source:

> In what could be the most decisive chapter yet in the saga, Westminster Council is gearing up for another legal challenge. Within weeks, lawyers for the borough will seek a fresh court order, which would require Dame Shirley to reveal for the first time the location of any assets transferred in the past. It would also freeze any remaining interest she had in them. The *Independent* understands that a date of

13th–15th February has been set for the case in the High Court. (*Independent*, 3 January 2003)

Angered by the Council's blatant attempts to persuade the media that it was chasing the Porter surcharge after being told to mind his own business a few months earlier, on 12 January 2003 Murad Qureshi wrote to the Chief Executive:

> I was disturbed to see a report in the *Independent* of 3rd January, showing in some detail the Council's hunt for the many millions Shirley Porter owes the Council and its residents. Given I was rebuked by Officers when asking similar questions at the last but one Finance Overview and Scrutiny Committee, I am troubled to see that elements of the media appear to know more than the relevant committee. Therefore I would appreciate if the leak would be investigated . . . It is one thing to suggest that members of the Committee could jeopardise the legal action by idle chat but quite another to find that either an arm of the Council or the agents we have employed have been leaking information which could enable Shirley Porter to move her assets once again in avoidance of paying the surcharge.

A month later, on 11 February, Qureshi received a dismissive reply from the chief executive: 'I am pleased to say that I have not found any evidence of confidential information being leaked from the City Council', blaming the *Independent* story on the papers stolen from court in January 2002 and reported in the *Daily Mirror* that month. Of course, much of the material in the *Independent* article was not included in the missing court papers of a year earlier.

A week after the *Independent* article, Council officers met a private investigator, George Liddell, employed by Cliff Stanford, a former business associate of John Porter. Stanford had hired Liddell to investigate Shirley Porter in the course of his board-room battle with John Porter over control of Redbus Interhouse.

Liddell offered the Council evidence of links between John Porter's financial affairs and those of his mother. However, the Council declined Liddell's offer on the grounds that Liddell wanted to be paid for the information and because they suspected that the information might have been stolen. In addition, the Council refused Liddell's information because, according to Colin Wilson, he and John Fordham 'chose to wait for Mr Liddell to make his information public'. The decision not to accept Liddell's gold-plated information until he went to the media, and also to claim it was too costly, further undermined the Council's commitment to a vigorous surcharge recovery process.

On 6 February, it was reported that Sir Leslie and Dame Shirley Porter were seventh in 'Britain's ten most generous philanthropists', with annual donations of £5.4 million. How that squared with Porter's claim that her assets amounted to just £300,000 is hard to fathom. A few days later, on 11 February, the High Court widened the definition of Porter's assets and froze them up to a value of £37 million. She was also required to provide wider disclosure. The deadline for this further disclosure was 18 February.

The next day, on 12 February, Keith Dovkants, one of the *Evening Standard*'s most experienced investigative reporters, contacted the Council's Press Office. According to the Council's note of the conversation Dovkants had with a Council press officer, 'he wants to write the definitive piece . . . No time pressure, he just wants to write the definitive piece.' Desperate to take advantage of any opportunity to get a positive story out to the media, the Council organised an interview for Dovkants with Fordham just two days later, on 14 February at 10.00 a.m.

The problem with the Council's strategy was that it required the Council to reveal confidential information about what it knew about Porter's finances and the actions it was planning. So, it was OK for the Council to reveal confidential information if it helped to restore the Council's tarnished reputation, but a 'crime' if others released confidential information in order to help the surcharge recovery.

The High Court decision of 18 February was significant for Porter. On that day, she got her solicitor to fax a letter from Israel to the chief executive to tell him:

Last November I was 72. I am no longer prepared to be immersed in the costs and emotions of a case which has now lasted a quarter of my adult life when the process seems so pointless and my family needs me more than ever. As a result I have decided not to participate in the latest proceedings any further. I remain extremely grateful for having had the opportunity of serving the people of Westminster and am proud of my achievements in public life. I have nothing more to add.

Remarkably, Peter Rogers did not reply to Porter's fax for over two months. He eventually got round to replying on 25 April, inviting her 'to make full disclosure under the Court order with which you have not so far complied and to put forward a proposal to settle this matter. If appropriate, our respective representatives could meet to discuss this. Until this matter is settled, further time and expense will be incurred by all concerned, including yourself.' This letter was sent to Porter's address in Tel Aviv by second class post (i.e. at inland rather than overseas rates) and did not arrive, according to her, until 1 July, a further two months later! Was this another example of the Council's vigorous recovery process?

On a more positive front, on 25 March 2003 disclosure orders were finally agreed by the High Court in respect of Peter Green, Porter's long-standing financial adviser. This was the first time that the Council had sought action against Green, despite being informed on numerous occasions by media reports, as far back as 1998, of his crucial role in moving Porter's assets.

But, at the same time, the Council continued its attempt to block the district auditor's public interest report, this time through a letter in the *Wood & Vale* newspaper from Rogers on 11 April, in which he argued that 'it would not be in the interests of Westminster taxpayers . . . and [the events] occurred as long as 15 years ago and Westminster Council has changed substantially since then. Westminster has moved on and these historical distractions should end.' This was followed on 12 May with a letter from Rogers to the district auditor's solicitors, arguing against the publication of the public interest report on the grounds of the cost of the surcharge recovery process. Rogers wrote: 'Since the House of Lords decision some £408,880 has been spent in pursuing the existing surcharge debts from Dame Shirley Porter and David Weeks, so far with virtually no financial return.'

So, with over £400,000 spent by the Council and not one penny piece having been paid by Porter, the Conservatives were desperate to put an end to this affair that had dogged them for over fifteen years. They clearly wanted to get out as quickly as possible. They had no real desire to collect the money. They were going through the motions, doing just enough to keep up appearances. But they were running out of steam. An analysis of the amount spent by the Council on legal costs since the December 2001 House of Lords' judgment reveals that, in the ten-month period up until early November 2002, the Council spent approximately £308,000, an average of £30,000 per month. However, in the following six months up to mid-May 2003, the Council's expenditure slowed down considerably. In the period from early November 2002 to mid-May 2003, the Council spent an additional £100,000 on legal costs, an average of around £16,000 a month, only just over half of the average monthly expenditure of the previous ten months. The amount spent on legal costs is an accurate reflection of the amount of effort put into the surcharge recovery process, as Stephenson Harwood were paid on an hourly basis.

18

Blowing the whistle on the Council's 'go slow'

A trail of spreadsheets and emails unearthed by a BBC investigation suggests that Dame Shirley Porter . . . is still exerting influence over a multimillion pound fortune, despite her pleas of poverty. The programme makers also claim to have personal emails suggesting that she has access to huge sums of money. In one message, Dame Shirley appears to write that she might have to spend $4 million (£2.5 million) to get her son 'out of trouble'.

Guardian, 30 June 2003

Thursday 8 May 2003 was a red letter day in the search for Shirley Porter's millions. What I was not to know was that it would also be the start of nearly two years of hell for my family and me. On that day, Karen Buck MP sent me a copy of the email she had received from George Liddell alleging wholesale failures in the Council's attempts to recover the surcharge owed by Porter and the Council's apparent lack of interest in the information Liddell was offering.

I was knocked sideways by the email and could not quite believe the enormity of what was being suggested. Part of me thought it might be the work of a crank. I had had no real day-to-day involvement in the discussions about collecting the surcharge, as this had been handled by Alan Lazarus and Simon Stockill as leaders of the Labour Group. I had wrongly assumed that, although the job of collecting the money from Porter was going to be difficult, the Council would do all it could, given the massive amounts involved. I suggested to Karen Buck that she pass the email to the Council's chief executive and ask for a response to the points made by Liddell.

Buck had also sent a copy of Liddell's email to Jonathan

Rosenberg and he, in turn, passed it to Andy Hosken of the BBC *Today* programme. Hosken had recently completed a *Today* investigation into Barry Legg which had resulted in Legg's resignation as Conservative Party chief executive. Rosenberg had helped Hosken with details of Legg's past role in the Council decision to house homeless families in the asbestos-ridden Hermes and Chantry Points on the Elgin estate in Paddington.

Six days later, on 14 May, I decided that I had an obligation myself to send the Liddell information to the Council. I sent the email to Peter Rogers, the chief executive, and copied it to Colin Wilson, director of Legal Services. On 16 May I received a confidential reply from Wilson's deputy, Donal Kerrigan, saying:

> We are well aware of Mr Liddell but have been proceeding with caution in relation to him. We have been collecting as much information as we properly could from him without committing the Council to a contract for his services and the fees he has clearly been trying to secure.

This seemed a very complacent response to me, given the allegations being made by Liddell. I was also bemused by the Council's refusal to pay for the vital information on offer. After all, the Council had had no obvious problems in paying private investigators for their work in the past.

I shared this information with Rosenberg and he suggested that we should meet with Hosken to discuss what it all meant and how we might cooperate in order to get to the bottom of what was going on. I was also determined that the Council would not wriggle out of its responsibilities of getting back the money owed by Porter. I hoped that working with the BBC again would prove as fruitful as it had back in 1989.

On the late afternoon of 22 May I met Hosken and Rosenberg at my office and I agreed to cooperate with Hosken on the basis that all information supplied to him would be on a deep background basis. Hosken then told me of his plans to meet Cliff Stanford, John Porter's former business partner, at his villa in Spain to discuss the information that Stanford had about the finances of John and Shirley Porter. He also agreed to give me any information that he got from Stanford that could be helpful to the Council in recovering the Porter surcharge, so that I could subsequently hand it over to the Council following its broadcast by the BBC. We then discussed Kerrigan's reply to me and a number of follow-up questions that I would ask.

On that same day Shirley Porter's application to the European Court of Human Rights was declared inadmissible. This decision finally ended Porter's legal battle. However, the judgment noted: 'Given that the applicant is now living out of the country and has failed to comply with the orders issued against her, the court would note that it appears the applicant has no intention of paying the surcharge, or any part of it, in any event.' The Council's view was that the verdict was largely academic. It looked like everyone had a pessimistic view of Porter's likelihood of paying up.

Little did I know that the Council was also making plans to throw in the towel. On 20 May 2003 Wilson wrote to John Fordham of Stephenson Harwood, responding to Fordham's request to increase his charging rates. Wilson believed that the Council was spending too much money, the prospects for recovering the surcharge were poor and it was time to consider calling a halt to the search for the Porter money. Wilson told Fordham:

> You will be aware of the City Council's concern about the mounting costs of this case, compared to the not too promising prospects of a substantial recovery. Accordingly, I should be grateful if you could do all that you can to ensure that, where ever practicable, work is delegated to the most junior member of the team, commensurate, of course, with maintaining proper standards. More generally, as you are aware, I am anxious that as soon as we sensibly can, we should provide a further report to Members on where we are and the future options, including a critical analysis of whether it makes any real sense to spend much more money on pursuing the debt.

Wilson's letter to Fordham was followed up on 2 June with a conversation with Rod Ainsworth of the Audit Commission. According to Wilson's own file note of the conversation:

I updated Rod generally on this matter and indicated that in the next 4–6 weeks or so I expected we would want to consult with him, as before, on a report on options to put before Members. Bearing in mind the considerable expenditure to date and the lack of substantial recovery, one option would clearly be to conclude that no further action should be taken.

On the same day Wilson also replied to my request for further information with a confidential note. However, some of the information contained in the note was clearly not confidential, a fact which immediately made me suspicious. Just over a week later, on 10 June, I met Hosken at a pub behind Holborn Underground station, five minutes' walk from my office. He showed me a number of documents that Stanford had given him just a few hours earlier at a meeting at Stanford's offices in Covent Garden. The documents were unbelievable! They comprised a number of emails and spreadsheets which demonstrated beyond doubt that John Porter had been investing his mother's money on her behalf and that his finances and his mother's were inextricably intertwined.

Now, knowing for certain that the Porters had been leading the Council a merry dance for years, I knew I was right to work with the BBC to expose the truth and force the Council to redouble its current lacklustre efforts to recover the £42 million debt. I gave Hosken a copy of the confidential note from Wilson. The note included reference to the disclosure orders which had been served against Shirley Porter's financial adviser, Peter Green, and the fact that no action was yet being taken against John Porter. The fact that no action was being taken against John Porter was extraordinary, given that the Council knew for a fact that Shirley Porter had sold her Hyde Park penthouse flat to John in 1994 for over £1 million, let alone what the emails revealed about the reality of their financial arrangements.

After consulting his BBC editorial and legal colleagues, over the following weeks Hosken requested me to ask more questions of the Council, including one about Green's compliance with the disclosure orders. I received a response almost immediately from Wilson, saying that 'he [Green] has complied [with the disclosure orders] and Messrs Stephenson Harwood are in the process of analysing the material'. However, it later emerged that, although Green had complied with the disclosure orders in the technical sense, i.e. he had made a declaration, the information he had provided was far from complete. Thankfully, using BBC information that I had provided after the *Today* programme on 30 June, the Council was later able to go back to the court to get a further disclosure order against Green.

Hosken and I continued our email correspondence. He wanted to get his facts totally accurate and the BBC lawyers wanted to make sure that everything was done correctly so that any broadcast could not be challenged. On 26 June I received a final request from him. Once again, I was reassured when he mentioned that the BBC lawyers were involved. I knew that they would not broadcast anything that could damage the Council's case.

On Friday 27 June Hosken told me that the programme would go out on Monday morning and that the BBC had made an arrangement with the *Times*, who would also publish the story on the same day. As we had arranged right from the outset, Hosken organised for the Stanford documents to be delivered to me, and on Sunday night Rosenberg acted as the BBC's courier and brought them round to my flat.

The next morning, 30 June, I woke up, had a shower and turned on the radio. At 7.30 a.m. Hosken's story went on air. His core argument was that the Council was not acting as quickly as it should have been to recover the £42 million surcharge owed by Shirley Porter. He told the *Today* listeners:

> By June, it was rumoured that the only items of worth recovered were a gold-plated toilet seat, two portraits of Dame Shirley she had commissioned herself, and a near-worthless half-share in a heavily mortgaged flat. It appeared to the outside world that she was cocking a snook at the rate-payers.

The programme quoted extensively from emails supplied by Stanford, showing that Porter's assets were very closely intertwined with those of her son, John. *Today* explained:

An investigation by this programme has revealed documents that appear to show her continuing to exert influence over the family fortune. Some of the documents we have obtained are personal emails written by Dame Shirley. These emails show the influence Dame Shirley has over the family's finances.

Here is a note from one email: 'All his [John Porter's] property is charged. Only the farm in Vermont is available, worth about $500,000. He requires about $2 million to get out of trouble, that will cost me $4 million. He is not liquid. I have asked for an account of his holdings and what security he will put up and when he will pay back.'

On February 11 this year Dame Shirley was ordered to disclose what interest she had in trusts. She has still failed to disclose anything in compliance with that order. The question remains: if Dame Shirley has a central role in influencing the family finances, as a prominent forensic accountant and QC we interviewed told us, why hasn't the Council widened its investigation to pursue third parties or other family members?

Email number 4, prepared in December 2000, shows Dame Shirley and her husband Sir Leslie as substantial investors in their son's company, called I-spire. These spreadsheets name two offshore companies, Whitecoast Investments Ltd and Sunset Trading Corporation. They indicate that, at the time, Whitecoast belonged to Dame Shirley and Sunset belonged to Sir Leslie.

Email number 5 was prepared by the family's financial advisers, PFM, entitled 'Porter Family Loans', showing that Whitecoast and Sunset lent either John Porter or his companies over $1.75 million during 2001. Our investigation has established that Whitecoast and Sunset are based in the British Virgin Islands, as are at least three other companies with clear links to the Porter family.

Hosken had gathered together an impressive string of expert witnesses. Michael Ash QC told the programme:

These documents, as far as one can see, indicate that control has been exercised over property which seems to have been either the property of trusts or companies . . . More than that one can hardly say but that's the indication.

Raj Belolia of Forensic Accounting said: 'Based on the documents you've shown me, she certainly appears to have a central role, she certainly appears to control or direct transfers of large amounts of monies. There is evidence of her being involved in significant transfers of funds.'

The report also included this passage: 'Senior council sources here at Westminster Council have told us that no action is currently being taken against the Porter family. Disclosure orders have not been issued against John Porter or other members of the family. The City Council currently has no basis for applying such orders.' The Council's later case against me revolved around their contention that the final sentence was confidential and its broadcast could, somehow, have helped Shirley Porter.

My next task was to arrange to hand over the Stanford material to the Council. So, just after 8.00 a.m., I emailed Peter Rogers to arrange an urgent meeting so that I could do this. During the course of the morning I arranged to go to City Hall for a 2.00 p.m. meeting.

Unbeknown to me, at 12.35 p.m. Rogers, Wilson, John Fordham of Stephenson Harwood, Rod Ainsworth of the Audit Commission and the Council's head of Communications, Alex Aiken, met to discuss the *Today* programme broadcast. As the note of that meeting makes crystal clear, their main collective concern was about how to minimise the bad publicity for the Council that the programme was already generating. They were all badly stung by Hosken's hard-hitting report. Interestingly, too, at no point during the meeting did any of those present make mention, discuss or raise any concern that an item of confidential information relating to John Porter had been broadcast by *Today*.

As arranged, at 2.00 p.m. I met Rogers in his sixteenth-floor office in City Hall with Wilson and Fordham and gave him all the documents that I had obtained from the BBC the previous evening. The meeting was cordial and matter-of-fact. No mention was made and no concerns were raised by Rogers or Wilson that part of the broadcast that morning had revealed confidential information about the action the Council was not taking against John Porter. Rogers, Wilson and Fordham appeared pleased to receive the documents and immediately made copies.

Later in the afternoon, Karen Buck and I met Stanford at the House of Commons. I finished the day with an email to the Director of Public Prosecutions to suggest that he took action against Shirley Porter for her contempt of court. Sadly, he did not even bother to reply. Nevertheless, it had been a busy day and I felt that we were about to make real progress.

The following morning, 1 July, *Today* broadcast a further item on the Council's search for Shirley Porter's assets, this time including an interview with Rogers. Rogers tried to put the Council's slow progress in context. He argued:

> I think it's important to set it in context. These events took place fifteen years ago so when people talk about eighteen months from the debt it needs to be set in the context of a fifteen-year programme. And what we have is somebody who is extremely wealthy, who has spent probably ten years prior to this moving money around, which makes it very complex and very costly to look at recovery processes.

During the interview, Sarah Montague asked Rogers: ' "Disclosure orders", this is a quote from the Council, "have not been issued against John Porter and other members of the family . . . the City Council has no basis for applying such orders." Is that still the case?'

Rogers was clearly rattled and replied:

> That is still our advice on the basis of the evidence that we have and what we will be doing is reviewing our evidence to see if we can tighten our controls against other members of the family and if we can secure that widening from the court process in the UK.

When I heard the exchange between Montague and Rogers my heart sank. I knew that the information that Montague had quoted had been marked 'confidential', even if it was, in my view, harmless. Indeed, the Adjudication Panel later agreed with me on this. But I knew that the Council would seize on it and come after me. I was also angry with the BBC. I had given the information on a deep background basis and I did not expect it to be broadcast word for word.

Shortly after I got to my office in Holborn that morning, I was contacted by Jean-Claude Depuis, a former client of Peter Green. Depuis was keen to get back at Green following bad business dealings with him and he offered new information which I believed could help the surcharge recovery process, including the fact that, according to Depuis, all Shirley Porter's sensitive papers are in Israel with her lawyer and that all her money is in a bank in Guernsey in Green's account. I immediately passed this information to the Council and, through Depuis, the Council was introduced to a former employee of Green, who was later able to confirm to the Council details of various movements of Porter's assets.

Later that day the inevitable happened. At 12.47 p.m. Wilson emailed me about 'a matter of serious concern' and proceeded to ask for my comments on that morning's *Today* programme and the passages read out by Montague, which 'appear to be a direct quote from my note to you accompanied by my email of 2nd June, both of which were clearly marked confidential'. Wilson also added what I considered the threatening comment that 'the Members' Code of Conduct clearly prohibits Members from disclosing information supplied to them in confidence and apparent breaches can be referred to the national Standards Board for investigation'.

The Council's plan of action was obvious. They would get their own back on me for revealing their go-slow so publicly by reporting me to the Standards Board for England. I decided that my best course of action was to deny everything, and so I replied at 1.07 p.m: 'I do not know where the *Today* programme got that information.' I knew, however, that from now on I was going to be in a very major battle with the Council and had better get myself in gear for a fight. I also decided that the best form of defence was attack. Not content to wait for the Council to tell me what they were doing with the valuable information I had given them the previous day, I demanded to know what they had done with it. As I had hoped, the response was positive and my cooperation with the BBC was yielding immediate results. Wilson told me:

We have read the documents you supplied us and will use such of
them/their contents as is appropriate in the pending applications and
in subsequent actions . . . we need to build a very strong case before
we can apply to the Court to freeze or otherwise lay our hands on the
assets of anyone other than Dame Shirley Porter herself . . . Your
documents are also relevant to building our case.

Wilson was actually playing down the usefulness of the
information I supplied. Indeed, it was used at once by the Council
to bolster Fordham's affidavit against Green. In a memo to Wilson
at 4.30 p.m. on 1 July, Fordham told Wilson that, following a
conversation with Counsel, 'we have provisionally concluded (if
it meets with your approval) that, in addition, we will exhibit the
Dimoldenberg material'. At 7.28 that evening Wilson replied: 'I
certainly agree that we should refer to the Dimoldenberg material
and possibly anything else useful from the BBC.'

The next day, the Council moved into top gear in its efforts to
cause me as much grief as possible, despite the invaluable use the
documents I had provided were proving in kick-starting the
search for Porter's money. That day, Emma Griffiths, a solicitor
from Stephenson Harwood, acting on behalf of the City Council,
visited the BBC Television Centre in Wood Lane, following a
request to the BBC, to inspect Andy Hosken's Porter files. In the
process, Griffiths discovered one item of confidential material
emailed by me to Hosken. This piece of information was copied
by Griffiths without Hosken's permission and subsequently given
to the City Council. The City Council later passed this piece of
paper to the Standards Board.

With this information the Council then moved in for the kill.
At 4.59 p.m. on Thursday 3 July, Wilson emailed me again:

You have said in your previous email that you do not know how the
Today programme got the information. I assume that you are saying
that none of the communications I have forwarded to you marked
'confidential' have been passed by you to the media. Is that correct? If
so, can you tell me please whether any such communications have
been passed to anyone else, even on a confidential basis, who might
have passed them on? Given that my email of 2nd June was not sent

by me to anybody else other than my Deputy Donal Kerrigan and the
Chief Executive, I am sure you will understand my concern and the
need for me to ask these questions. The publication of confidential
information about what we are or are not doing in relation to this case
could obviously prejudice our efforts to secure recovery.

Of course, Wilson failed to reveal to me the information from the
BBC in his possession. Normally, I would have given my response
to Wilson very careful thought, but on this occasion, I was
clearing my desk and about to go away for a long weekend and
not returning until late on the following Monday. I also knew
that, as soon as I admitted that I had passed confidential information to the BBC, the Council would try to get its own back on
me for exposing their dilatory performance by going straight to
the Standards Board to get me thrown off the Council. So, I
decided to continue to deny everything and replied half an hour
later, at 5.32 p.m.: 'I can confirm that none of the documents sent
to me by you marked confidential have been passed by me to the
media or anyone else.'

Of course, I had no idea then that the Council had been
through Hosken's files at the BBC and had removed the one piece
of evidence that proved my reply to be incorrect.

The following Monday, 7 July, Simon Stockill, leader of the
Labour Group, and Labour chief whip Barrie Taylor were
summoned to a meeting with Wilson and Peter Rogers. Stockill
and Taylor were briefed on the confidential document found by
Stephenson Harwood in the BBC files and Rogers's intention to
report me to the Standards Board for breaching the Code of
Conduct. Immediately following the meeting both Stockill and
Taylor phoned me to brief me on the meeting.

The next day, I phoned Rogers to discuss his intention to refer
me to the Standards Board. His response was to tell me that
neither Stockill nor Taylor should have told me of the details of
the previous night's meeting as it was a confidential meeting. At
this point I thought I would give Rogers a dose of his own
medicine. I said to him that, having been told that Councillors
Stockill and Taylor had revealed confidential information to me,
he had no option but to also report them both to the Standards

Board, too, for breaching the Code of Conduct! Later that day, Rogers informed me that, having consulted with the director of Legal and Administrative Services, he had concluded, conveniently, that he had not made it sufficiently clear to Stockill and Taylor that the previous night's meeting was confidential. In the circumstances, therefore, he informed me that there was no requirement to report those councillors to the Standards Board! There was more of this Alice in Wonderland logic to follow from the Council as the weeks and months unfolded.

On 9 July, just six working days after the *Today* broadcasts, the Council secured a breakthrough which was to prove very significant in the search for Porter's money. On that day the Council successfully secured freezing orders on those parts of John Porter's assets intertwined with those of his mother. Wilson later admitted that the freezing order 'was obtained on the basis of both the Stanford/Liddell evidence and evidence from other sources'. Indeed, an affidavit sworn by Fordham revealed that 'documents were made available to the Council both at the BBC and also copies were provided to the Council's legal team by one of its councillors. The information contained in them raises very serious concerns as to the truthfulness of the affidavit evidence of DSP'.

For whatever reason, the Council did not reveal the existence of the freezing orders against John Porter until November 2003. I did not expect any thanks from the Council for the information that I had provided, but I believe that it was inexcusable for the Council to continue to maintain that what I had done might have prejudiced the Council's surcharge recovery prospects. The opposite was the truth. My actions had helped to breathe life into a case which was on its last legs and which the Council were about to drop.

On 9 July, I also made a last ditch appeal to Rogers setting out why I believed a complaint to the Standards Board would be totally inappropriate. I told him:

> First, for the past 15 years I have displayed a total and unswerving commitment to seek the truth about the 'Homes for Votes' scandal. This is in stark contrast to members of the Majority Party over the years. As you know, I wrote to Mr Phillips on numerous occasions in

the late 1980s to seek the truth, only to be met by evasions. There can be no doubt that I have the very highest motives in this matter. I acted as a 'whistleblower' and helped to expose the wrongdoing perpetrated by members of the Council. I have been on the right side of this argument from day one.

Second, in recent weeks I have been totally helpful to the Council's task of recovering the money owed by Porter and Weeks. I passed on the information supplied by George Liddell to Karen Buck MP about the people and companies that have been working in concert with Porter. I also passed on to you a large bundle of information that I acquired about the Porter family's financial and other dealings the day that these issues were broadcast by the *Today* programme. The Council has saved itself thousands of pounds by my detailed and close involvement in passing on information to you at no cost.

In any event no harm has been done to the Council's case. I believe that the test of whether this matter should be referred to the Standards Board is twofold – (a) whether my motives were designed to damage the Council and (b) whether any harm has been done to the Council. On both matters I believe the answer to be no.

Rogers was unmoved by my arguments and claimed that he had 'no choice' in whether or not to refer his complaint to the Standards Board. He claimed that he had no discretion in the matter. Rogers also told me that he would ask the Standards Board not to refer the complaint back to the Council's Standards Committee. He knew that I would not get a fair hearing by the Conservatives, given the history of 'Homes for Votes' within the City Council.

I was feeling more under threat as every day that passed. So much so that on 14 July I wrote to Sir Andrew Foster, controller of the Audit Commission, to express my concerns and that I felt 'intimidated by the City Council who, I believe, are trying to "frighten me off the case"'. The Council's double standards were further highlighted by a strictly confidential email sent on the same day by Wilson to his senior legal staff. He told them:

In connection with the Dame Shirley Porter matter, we have prima facie evidence that Cllr Dimoldenberg has forwarded confidential material given to him on that basis and as a councillor, to the media. The Chief Executive is currently considering a reference to the Standards Board for England in respect of this apparent breach of the Members Code of Conduct.

The purpose of this email is to make you aware so that if Councillor Dimoldenberg asks you for confidential information on any other matter you can consider it in the context of the above and discuss with me/the Chief Executive as necessary.

I am not suggesting that you refuse him all and any confidential material. Where Cllr Dimoldenberg is working constructively with the City Council, as he is on a number of issues, there may be no harm in giving him the material. On the other hand, where we are aware that he is opposing the City Council on an issue, and harm to the City Council's interests could result from publication of the material he has asked for, we may need to refuse him access. Chief Officers have been so advised.

The existence of this email was not discovered until I was able to go through the material that the Council had disclosed to the Standards Board in early 2005! No wonder the Council wanted to keep from me the double standards to which they were working. What Wilson's memo was effectively saying was that I could have any information I liked if this was in pursuit of 'working constructively with the City Council'. But if they thought I was 'opposing the City Council' I was to get nothing. The irony of my situation was that I believed my actions were completely constructive and totally consistent with the Council's job of recovering the £42 million Porter surcharge!

19

The Council calls in the Standards Board

Because of the political sensitivity of this matter, it is certainly not beyond the realms of possibility that someone may seek to suggest that the complaint has been made in an attempt to 'gag' Councillor Dimoldenberg in his efforts to expose the City Council's, he would argue, lack of resolve and progress in pursuing the debt owed by Dame Shirley Porter and David Weeks. This is certainly not the case, but in the circumstances it would be very helpful to have this matter disposed of as quickly as possible.

Letter of complaint sent by the City Council to the
Standards Board for England, 18 July 2003

On 18 July 2003 Peter Rogers made a formal complaint to the Standards Board alleging that I leaked confidential information to the press. Rogers was clearly alive to the public perception of what he was doing and wanted it to be dealt with quickly so that any bad publicity for the City Council could be minimised. With typical Westminster efficiency, Rogers's letter of complaint did not reach the Standards Board until 6 August, nearly three weeks later, because the Council wrongly addressed the letter.

At this point, you may be wondering what the Standards Board is, who they are and what they do. Set up by the Local Government Act 2000, the Standards Board for England was the Labour government's attempt to rid local government of sleaze following bad experiences across the country – in places such as Doncaster, Hackney and, of course, Westminster. The new rules for local government required all councillors to sign up to and adhere to a new Code of Conduct. This code was aimed at promoting the highest standards of behaviour and conduct throughout local government through a system of penalties for those who were found guilty of transgressing it. For example, failure to declare all interests, financial or otherwise, would be reported to the Standards Board for investigation and the penalty, for those found guilty, was suspension or disqualification from the council. One particular aspect of the code outlawed the release of confidential information. Another part of it was a catch-all provision which could lead to suspension or disqualification for actions or behaviour which might 'bring the Council into disrepute'. Suspension or disqualification would be handed out to those found to be in the wrong by the sinisterly titled Adjudication Panel for England, to which all cases of suspected code-breaking were to be referred by the Standards Board.

Sadly, however, the government's good intentions did not turn out as expected. A flavour of the problems ahead could have been foreseen by the parliamentary debates as the legislation was working its way through the House of Commons. On 8 June 2000, Beverley Hughes MP, the local government minister and hence responsible for the Bill, responded to an intervention from Don Foster MP, the Liberal Democrat spokesman: 'How many times is the Adjudication Panel likely to be required to set up a case tribunal? Clearly she does not know the precise number, but can she tell us the order of magnitude?'

Hughes clearly did not expect the new legislation to uncover a great mass of corrupt behaviour in local government and gave the perfectly reasonable reply that

> at the moment the number of serious cases is relatively small and declining, so we can expect that the full panoply of the process, leading to the establishment of a tribunal, would be necessary only a few times a year. That is a reasonable prediction on the basis of the current situation and recent trends.

Unfortunately for Hughes, and for local government generally, her reasonable prediction on the evidence of the recent past turned out be massively understated. The new system generated an average of 100 Adjudication Panel meetings a year from January 2003 onwards.

According to the Standards Board's statistics, the new

legislation resulted in around 3,500 complaints a year against councillors (an average of seventy per week), of which two-thirds were rejected as being inappropriate for investigation. Speaking at the Standards Board annual conference on 13 September 2004, Sir Brian Briscoe, chief executive of the Local Government Association, said: 'In my view, there was not enough scrutiny of the legislation in either House. This framework is still flawed. [The Act has bred] a cynical view about the board and its performance.' It is hard to deny Briscoe's damning conclusions.

Dissatisfaction with the Standards Board finally came to a head on 19 January 2005, when the Committee on Standards in Public Life published its tenth report, including the results of its investigations into the operations of the Standards Board. The report concluded that there were fundamental and structural weaknesses in the way in which the Standards Board operated and that it needed significant changes if it is to operate in a way which wins public trust and embeds an ethical culture into our public bodies.

The committee also reported on 'whistleblowing': 'Effective whistleblowing is a key component in any strategy to challenge inappropriate behaviour at all levels of an organisation. It is both an instrument in support of good governance and a manifestation of a more open organisational culture.'

But now that the Standards Board process was running, I had to deal with it. On 13 August 2003 I asked the Standards Board for a copy of the chief executive's letter of complaint against me. They refused. I tried again and again to get the details of the charges against me and the evidence from the Council and the Standards Board, but on every occasion I was turned down. I finally received a copy of Rogers's original letter on 20 January 2004 – over five months after it was sent.

The ethical standards officer assigned to my case was a Nick Marcar. Searching through the Standards Board's web site I found out that Marcar joined the Standards Board in January 2002 and appeared to have no experience of local government: 'Marcar has over twenty years' experience of civil investigations with the Department of Trade and Industry. A member of the Chartered Association of Certified Accountants, he was responsible for some of the largest investigations of corporate fraud and insider dealing undertaken by the DTI.'

My heart sank further. What did this man know about local government, local politics or Westminster? Had he ever heard of Shirley Porter or the district auditor? If I asked him about selling cemeteries for 15p, would he think I was mad? I was slightly cheered, however, by reading the 'Guide to Standards Board Investigations', which was included with letter. It said: 'Local newspapers have an important role to play in maintaining the transparency of local administration.' Yes, I would agree completely with the important role of the media, but somehow I doubted whether they would accept that as my defence.

I began to think about getting legal advice. My first thought was to talk to Neale Coleman. He had helped Ken Livingstone in his recent brush with the Standards Board and had instructed Tony Childs, John Magill's legal adviser. Coleman suggested I ask Childs if he could advise me. I spoke to Childs but he said he was conflicted because the district auditor's public interest report had yet to be published. He suggested I approach Leonie Cowen, Camden's former director of Law, who was now in private practice. In late September I called Cowen and she agreed to advise me.

On 27 November 2003 I was interviewed for three hours by both Marcar and Paul McGowan, the Standards Board investigator. They spent a lot of time setting up the complicated tape-recording machinery, similar to what you see in police dramas when they are interviewing murder suspects. That in itself is unnerving. At the very start of the interview, I was asked by McGowan: 'Is there anything you'd like to tell me about the original allegation?' I had decided that there was no point in denying what I had done any longer and so I replied: 'I would. I would like to apologise unreservedly for any breach of the Code of Conduct.'

I had prepared a written defence of what I had done, why I had done it and the positive outcome so far. I sensed that Marcar and McGowan were not at all interested in what I had to say. They did ask, however, for copies of all emails I had sent from my Council and work personal computers relating to Porter. Not being expert about these things I had no idea what was possible. So, after talking it over with Cowen, I asked them to write to me with full details of what was required.

I also got a real sense that neither Marcar nor McGowan had any idea of who Porter was or of the significance of the 'Homes for Votes' scandal. In local government terms, they were amateurs. At the end of the interview, Marcar told me: 'Nothing stops you from providing information to us in whatever format you wish to.' And McGowan added: 'If you feel following today's meeting there's something new comes to your attention or, you think about, you're entitled to provide us with that information.' I took that as a genuine request for more information. However, as I took them at their word over the coming months and sent them a series of additional papers, I was later accused by them both of repeatedly trying to justify my actions and therefore compounding my crimes. It was truly Kafkaesque.

Following the Standards Board grilling I spent the next few weeks frantically trying to retrieve emails that were almost six months old. Not surprisingly, the Council's system could not provide everything I needed to respond fully to the Standards Board's request. I sent copies of what the Council could recover together with paper copies of emails sent from my Good Relations computer. However, that did not stop the Standards Board pursuing me further, and on 20 January 2004 I received a letter requesting copies of fourteen emails sent by me from my Good Relations computer.

To add insult to injury, on the same day I also received a package from the Standards Board enclosing a copy of Rogers's letter of complaint against me from 18 July 2003. The covering letter informed me that the letter of complaint 'has been released in order to assist you to answer the allegations you face under the code of conduct'. It is a pity that I received this key piece of information nearly two months after I had been interviewed by the Standards Board's investigating officers.

Having very belatedly given me Rogers's original letter, the Standards Board continued to harass me for copies of emails that had long been deleted. At the same time, all the extra information that I had supplied to them at their request following my

November grilling was effectively labelled 'garbage'. On 4 February I received a letter from McGowan telling me: 'To date I have received no information showing all emails relating to DSP, although I have received copious amounts of correspondence from you not relevant to my investigation.'

Things continued to get worse and on 20 February the Standards Board tightened their grip on me when McGowan wrote: 'I acknowledge that you have provided some, but not all of the information originally requested in my letter of 5 December . . . As a result, I have decided that it is necessary for me to write, in confidence, to the Managing Director of Good Relations in relation to the information concerned.' Not content with making life difficult for me at the Council, the Standards Board now wanted to extend their inquiries into my work and directly involve my boss. Thankfully, Annie Fossey, the managing director at Good Relations, gave me 100 per cent support throughout this ordeal.

20

The search for Porter's money finally moves into top gear

Stephenson Harwood, the City lawyers pursuing her, were helped by the work of another investigator, George Liddell, who had obtained information about financial dealings between her and her son. The trail took the lawyers to Guernsey, Switzerland, Bermuda, the British Virgin Islands, a backstreet lawyer in Panama City, and to potential property deals in Nashville, Tennessee. They even looked at a housing development in Birmingham to see if there was a connection with a land investment made by a Porter family trust.

According to Mr Liddell, the Guernsey bank account numbers were kept in a notebook by a trustee who slept with it under his pillow.

Guardian, 5 November 2005

The *Today* programme's broadcast of Cliff Stanford's information had an instant and positive impact on the Council's surcharge recovery activities. The information that I had handed over to the Council on 30 June 2003 was immediately used in the preparation of High Court affidavits against Peter Green and John Porter.

The Audit Commission also became more actively involved in policing the recovery process and on 24 July 2003 a meeting was held between the City Council, Stephenson Harwood, the district auditor and the Audit Commission to review progress. The note of the meeting revealed that 'the issue of cost is paramount to WCC's assessment of how much further the matters can be taken'. So, despite having been handed over the valuable Stanford/Liddell information for free, the Council was still quibbling over costs.

On 18 July the Urgency Committee of the Cabinet met for only the second time since the House of Lords' judgment in December 2001. The committee had last met on 6 November 2002 – a gap of over nine months. But activity was now increasing dramatically. In the seven-week period from 30 June to 18 August, the Council had spent the huge sum of £195,000 on legal costs, compared with £425,000 in the nineteen months between mid-December 2001 and 30 June 2003, and had been in court thirteen times as against twenty-three times during the earlier period.

The report of the Urgency Committee meeting gave details of the information that had been obtained as a result of disclosure orders. Significantly, however, it also revealed for the first time that the Council had been considering pulling the plug on the recovery process prior to the *Today* programme:

> The original intention was for the information disclosed by the orders to be reported to this committee prior to any further substantive steps being taken, in order that the cost/benefit of such further steps could be assessed by Members. However, recent events involving the publication in the media of information from documents, such as emails between [Shirley Porter] and her son John . . . required an urgent re-evaluation of the situation.

On 22 August, Colin Wilson, the Council's director of Legal Services, told me: 'The provision of information was certainly useful . . . I am happy to confirm that there has been intense legal activity in the period following the *Today* programme.' He followed that up with the news, on 26 August, that 'considerable progress has been made' and the next day he told me: 'I am not aware of any specific set-back that I would attribute to the *Today* programme.'

Following *Today*, the Council also invested in 'forensic computing'. They hired a company called Vogon International to take complete images of the hard disks contained in Green's computers. These images were then processed and forensic recovery techniques were used to analyse Green's deleted files. This provided vital evidence for the Council. But the question has to be asked, why did they wait until after the *Today* programme to take this obvious step?

By early November 2003, the Council was able to report further substantial progress and issued a press release, prior to 5 November's confidential meeting of the Urgency Committee of the Cabinet, reporting: 'Investments and cash have been frozen in bank accounts, and a freezing order has also been granted in respect of any of Dame Shirley's assets held by her son, John. The assets disclosed as a result of the Court orders have a value of many millions of pounds.'

The Council was also now spending considerably more on legal costs than before – another indication that the recovery process was in top gear. Indeed, the Council's legal bills more than doubled – from £425,848 for the eighteen-month period December 2001–June 2003 to £1,063,986 over the next five months (June–November 2003), following the *Today* programme and subsequent media coverage. And slowly, too, the Council began to acknowledge the help that had been given by the BBC and the media generally.

On 7 November John Fordham of Stephenson Harwood told the *Wood & Vale*: 'I think that the overall process has been assisted by the media. That material has formed part of our total knowledge and has been very useful.' Four days later he commented to the *Times* that 'the leaks to the press were one of our starting points'. Even Peter Rogers, the chief executive, had to admit my role had been helpful. He wrote to me on 20 November to say: 'There is no doubt that the fact that certain material was put in the public domain did assist us in being able to use that material. I fully acknowledge and appreciate the information that you have provided which has supported the Council's case . . . This has advanced the prospects of recovery.' That, however, did not stop him from continuing to try to prevent publication of the district auditor's public interest report. On 10 December he wrote again to John Magill's solicitor to inform him that the City Council 'is concerned that, in practice, the issue of a Public Interest Report will, at least in the short term, resurrect issues which are now purely historical and may, in fact make it more difficult for the City Council to draw a line under the past'.

Progress continued into the New Year, and, at the Urgency Committee's meeting on 9 February 2004, it was agreed to take the significant step to write to Shirley Porter to propose mediation. News, however, of this suggestion did not surface until the next month, when the *Sunday Telegraph* reported that Porter had offered £10 million to settle her £42 million surcharge bill.

On 8 March the Urgency Committee of the Cabinet met again and agreed a strategy for the mediation negotiations. Authority to settle was given to Rogers, in consultation with Wilson and Fordham. The stage was set for a deal to be done.

But before that, time for another twist to this extraordinary tale.

21

The signed, undated letter of resignation

I had spoken to the Leader of the Opposition and the Chief Whip, who were both concerned regarding the impact that this case was having on Cllr Dimoldenberg and . . . his family. . . . I was conscious that there was no end in sight from the Standards Board and was keen if possible to secure a solution for the benefit of the Council and for Cllr Dimoldenberg himself. I therefore suggested to Cllr Stockill that it may be possible for me to withdraw my objection if I received an undated letter of resignation from Cllr Dimoldenberg which I would exercise in the event of any similar confidential disclosure in the future.

Peter Rogers, letter to the Standards Board for England,
28 April 2004

There were many twists and turns in the 'Homes for Votes' saga but one of the most extraordinary events took place in early December 2003. Following a meeting between Peter Rogers, Simon Stockill and Barrie Taylor, Stockill emailed Rogers on 9th December:

Following our phone discussion last week, I have had a discussion with Barrie as Group Whip and some time to think over your proposal to offer to withdraw your referral of Paul to the [Standards Board] in return for an undated resignation letter from him.

It seems to me that the suggestion has no merit . . . I cannot really understand how you have the discretion to withdraw the referral now when you maintained you did not have the discretion to avoid a referral initially.

As Stockill explained it, the undated, signed resignation letter from me would be used by Rogers at any time in the future if he considered that I had broken the Code of Conduct. This was a quite bizarre suggestion and probably unprecedented in local government history. How Rogers could have thought that such a suggestion could possibly have been lawful is beyond belief. As an experienced chief executive, it is staggering that such a thought could have even crossed his mind.

Peter Rogers joined the City Council as head of Finance and Support Services on 28 March 1996. He had previously been commercial director of West Midlands Travel, which was sold to its employees in December 1991 for £70.7 million. Just over three years later, in March 1995, West Midlands Travel was bought by National Express for £243 million, handing a windfall to the company's 5,000 employee shareholders, who owned an average of 12,000 shares each and saw the value of their holdings triple to around £30,000. As commercial director, Rogers's windfall would have been considerably more than the average £30,000.

It would be an understatement to say that I was outraged by Rogers's proposal to supply him with a signed, undated letter of resignation from the Council in return for him dropping the case against me. On 7 January 2004, I wrote to the new district auditor, Derek Elliott, to ask for his views. He did not want to get involved and replied eight days later to say that it was none of his business:

> It is not my role as auditor to offer advice to individual members of the Council. It would therefore not be appropriate for me to comment on the specific matter which you have raised. The Standards Board for England is responsible for promotion of ethical conduct. It appears to me that any enquiry is more appropriately directed to the Standards Board.

Of course, Elliott must have known that the Standards Board only deals with the conduct of councillors, not Council officials. Nevertheless, on 22 January, as Elliott advised, I wrote to John Edwards of the Standards Board, about Rogers's suggested signed, undated letter of resignation, to see what sort of response I would get. True to form, a week later on 29 January, Edwards replied in exactly the terms I was expecting: 'The Standards Board cannot consider allegations about the conduct of officers of local authorities . . . Accordingly, we will not be considering the conduct of the Chief Executive.' More interesting, however, was the additional information provided by Edwards that, even if Rogers or anyone else wanted to halt the investigation against me, they could not do it. Once an investigation has started it must, by law, continue, come what may.

It wasn't until 28 April that Rogers explained his actions – under pressure from the Standards Board to account for his extraordinary behaviour. He explained:

> I had spoken to the Leader of the Opposition and the Chief Whip, who were both concerned regarding the impact that this case was having on Cllr Dimoldenberg and, indeed, his family. In their view it was this concern that was causing Cllr Dimoldenberg to lash out and was causing the sort of behaviour that we were experiencing. I was conscious that there was no end in sight from the Standards Board and was keen if possible to secure a solution for the benefit of the Council and for Cllr Dimoldenberg himself. I therefore suggested to Cllr Stockill that it may be possible for me to withdraw my objection if I received an undated letter of resignation from Cllr Dimoldenberg which I would exercise in the event of any similar confidential disclosure in the future.
>
> I thought my conversations were only exploratory with the Leader and Whip of the Opposition Party, and I am surprised that they have been discussed with Cllr Dimoldenberg.
>
> It was not my intention to put pressure on Cllr Dimoldenberg to resign, indeed the resignation would only have been triggered by a future breach of standards; my intention was to resolve the considerable waste of public time that we were experiencing and to relieve pressure on Cllr Dimoldenberg in view of the time that the investigation was taking.

On 3 February John Magill, the former district auditor, published his long-awaited public interest report. Tellingly, he found that the senior officers involved were prepared to lend their support to policies of a party political character which were not in the interests of the Council's taxpayers as a whole. The conduct of those then leading Members and senior officers, who were aware that those policies were formulated in order to promote the electoral advantage of the Conservative Party, yet were party to the consequent misuse of public resources, fell a long way short of the standards of conduct expected of those in public life and warrants criticism.

In particular, the public interest report looked closely at Council enforcement policies, the subject of a report by the current chief whip, Robert Davis, back in the late 1980s. In his report Magill concluded:

I consider that the proposals in that paper, that enforcement resources should be concentrated in line with [Building Stable Communities] strategy in our target wards, ensuring that the right type of homes are provided bringing with it the right sort of voters and questioning the use of limited enforcement resources in two of the safest seats in Westminster, indicate that the paper was proposing the use of Council resources for an improper purpose.

Although the district auditor did not find sufficient evidence that Davis's proposals were implemented, he did find that

other [later] documentation satisfies me that some enforcement activity was targeted in the key/marginal wards as a contribution towards meeting the electoral targets for those wards. Accordingly, it appears to me that the Council incurred [unlawful] net expenditure in that respect and that there is a loss in the Council's accounts.

Magill concluded: 'In my view, the conduct of those officers and Members who were aware of such targeting [of enforcement policies] directed at marginal wards in order to promote the electoral advantage of the Conservative Party fell well short of the standard expected and warrants criticism.'

Unsurprisingly, Davis and the Council leader, Simon Milton, and their Conservative colleagues and Council officers chose to ignore this damning conclusion. Instead, the Conservatives and Council officers concentrated on Magill's final words on the subject urging everyone to draw a line under the 'Homes for Votes' events.

So it was no surprise whatsoever when, on 17 March 2004, the City Council met to debate the district auditor's public interest report and agreed to take no further action. Clearly under severe pressure because of the unambiguous criticism from the district auditor, Milton went into great detail to explain his involvement in the fateful and unforgivable decision to house homeless families in asbestos-ridden flats.

In sombre tones he searched the recesses of the past and told the Council:

> In February 1989 I had been a councillor for ten months – the newest and youngest member of the council with no official position of responsibility . . . My presence at Chairmen's Group was therefore unusual. One month earlier, in January 1989, I had been asked by the then chief whip to act as a Council liaison officer between the Council [Conservative] group and the two [Conservative] associations with a view to ensuring that good news stories about the Council and its policies were disseminated in the run-up to the 1990 elections. It was thought that being allowed to observe the discussion of policy would facilitate this.

Denying any suggestions that the plans were inspired by party political considerations, he claimed: 'The proposal to use the Points as temporary accommodation came, not from any councillor, but from the Housing Department.' However, far from being the political novice he claims to have been in 1989, Milton, a graduate of Cambridge and Cornell Universities, had been a Conservative activist all his adult life.

22

Porter settles for £12.3 million – but what about the other £30 million?

Dame Shirley Porter has got off lightly by agreeing to pay £12 million to Westminster City Council in final settlement of her liability in the homes-for-votes scandal. The agreed settlement is less than half of the original surcharge and a third of what is currently owing. How would Westminster react if its less wealthy residents offered to pay a third of their council tax?

Wood & Vale, 30 April 2004

At midday on Saturday 24 April I heard from Simon Stockill that at 3.00 p.m. the Council would be telling the media that they had done a deal with Porter and would settle for £12.3 million. Stockill had received a call from an ecstatic Peter Rogers, who had just landed back from Brussels, where the deal had been done on the Friday night. My reactions to this news were going in many different directions. On the one hand, I was delighted that Shirley Porter had been forced to pay back over £12 million. On the other, I knew she was worth a great deal more and was getting off relatively lightly. I knew too that it would now be very difficult for the Council or the Standards Board to maintain that my actions had in any way damaged the Council's recovery prospects.

The Council's press machine now went into overdrive, with deputy leader Kit Malthouse telling everyone that 'I believe that this is a good settlement for the Council' and John Fordham patting himself on the back and claiming: 'In my judgement it is an excellent result.' On 26 April, Rogers followed up with a letter to all Council staff to tell them: 'I believe this is as good a settlement as the Council could obtain. The Audit Commission has supported our approach throughout the negotiations and shares our view of the final sum.'

Porter's statement to the press, however, was in typical denial mode. She told the world: 'I have decided that it is time to bring this case to an end, despite my belief that I did nothing wrong. As leader of the Council I was repeatedly assured that the policies we followed were lawful.'

The Council's negotiating position was that Porter was very rich and could afford to pay at least £30 million. And that raises the question, why did the Council settle for less than half of that amount?

We knew that this was the Council's weak spot when Malthouse could only respond to these points with personal abuse. Typical was his response to Peter Bradley MP's comment that Porter 'will be laughing all the way to an unnumbered Swiss bank account' (House of Commons debate, 30 June 2004). Malthouse, an old-school 'political bruiser', described Bradley as 'one of the Shirley Porter obsessives who have had very little in their lives for the past 18 years and find it very difficult to let it go'.

The full Council met on 12 May and was asked merely to note the settlement with Porter. It was also revealed that night that £1,735,473 had been spent by the Council on the costs of the Porter surcharge recovery. Since the *Today* programme on 30 June 2003, the Council had spent approximately £1.3 million on legal costs, an average of £124,000 per month. This compares with the average monthly expenditure on legal costs of £30,000 for the period January 2002–November 2002 and just £16,000 per month for the period immediately before the *Today* programme, from November 2002 to mid-May 2003. There could be no doubt that *Today* had acted as a supersonic 'rocket' under the Council.

The Council was also told that, of the £12 million which had been recovered, approximately half would be deducted to cover current and past legal costs. Details of the settlement were included in an appendix to the report which, conveniently for Porter, was 'subject to confidentiality provisions'. Later,

Malthouse justified the secrecy by claiming: 'If the settlement had not been confidential then the family's details would have been released, which would have been unfair' (*Wood & Vale*, 3 September 2004).

In essence, the decision to reach an agreement with Porter was delegated to a single Council officer, Rogers, in consultation with Malthouse, Colin Wilson, director of Legal and Administrative Services, and Stephenson Harwood, the Council's legal advisers. Only three other councillors were given details of the terms of the settlement agreement. Even the members of the Cabinet Urgency Committee were simply asked to note the settlement agreement. None of the other fifty-six members of the Council was given details of the settlement and no vote was taken at the Council meeting on 12 May 2004.

In an age of supposed transparency and open government it was completely unacceptable to close the final chapter on the biggest local government scandal in British history in such a secretive manner. To add a further insult, the settlement agreement also included a 'shredding clause', whereby Westminster agreed to either destroy all the Porter documents in their possession or hand them over to Porter's solicitors seven days after the money had been received. Just to make sure all the damning evidence was destroyed, Westminster chose the shredder.

With the settlement now agreed, on 25 April 2004 I wrote to the Standards Board to suggest that they close their investigations into Rogers's complaint against me as it was 'beyond doubt that none of my actions have in any way damaged the City Council's recovery of the surcharge owed by Dame Shirley Porter'. I followed this up with a letter to Rogers to suggest that he write to the Standards Board to recommend that they take no further action on his complaint. The next day Rogers replied in his downbeat fashion, 'I do not intend to withdraw my complaint – but I will make sure the Standards Board knows the outcome of the settlement.'

Two months later, on 28 June, Rogers told the Standards Board:

Last week the courts of the BVI [British Virgin Islands] approved the actions necessary to complete the settlement agreed by the Council with Dame Shirley Porter and her family. The settlement is regarded by both the Council and the Audit Commission as a good one. The actions which I referred for investigation which were taken by Cllr Dimoldenberg do not therefore appear to have damaged the Council's settlement prospects.

The Standards Board appeared, however, to be living in a world of its own. On 26 April, Nick Marcar, the board's ethical standards officer, wrote to me to say: 'We are reaching the end of our investigation and I expect to be in a position to send you a draft of my report during the course of May.' However, it later appeared that he had not even bothered to contact Andy Hosken at the BBC until he wrote to him on 4 May requesting copies of various confidential documents. Hosken refused to give Marcar the information. But to underline the importance Marcar attached to Hosken's information, he wrote to him again on 28 May to press for the information. How the Standards Board could claim on 26 April that they were 'reaching the end of our investigation' when they had not even contacted the BBC must throw into question the professional competence of those running such investigations.

Throughout the period that the Standards Board investigation had been running, almost twelve months, I had received tremendous support from the Labour Group, Labour Party members and political friends, as well of course from my family. I could not have got through the ordeal without them all. It had not been my intention to seek re-election as leader of the Labour Group (once was enough, thank you) but when Simon Stockill decided to stand down for work reasons, Barrie Taylor and others suggested that a very public way for the group to express its support for me would be to elect me as the new leader. By this time I was focused on proving my innocence and the prospect of another platform from which to argue my case was very appealing. I accepted the nomination and was elected unopposed on 14 June 2004. I was looking forward to the challenge of leading the Labour Group once again and my new position recharged my overworked batteries.

Two weeks later, on 30 June 2004, I was brought back down to earth. The Standards Board finally published its draft report and concluded that I had broken Parts 3(a) and 4 of the Code of Conduct – i.e. that I had leaked confidential information and had brought the Council into disrepute. The report was riddled with errors and omissions. For example, it missed out any reference to the fact that the Council had reached a £12.3 million settlement with Porter or that the settlement had been described as 'good' by the City Council and the Audit Commission. To rub salt into the wounds, the next day I received an email from Wilson informing me that the Council had 'just received confirmation that our bank has received the £12.3 million pursuant to the settlement agreement'.

The Council hoped against hope that this would be an end to the Porter 'Homes for Votes' saga. On 6 July, Malthouse told the *Independent*: 'As far as I am concerned this can be filed, archived and forgotten.' But the affair doggedly continued to maintain its high profile when, the next day, Karen Buck MP intervened at Prime Minister's Questions to ask Tony Blair: 'Will my Right Honourable Friend join me in congratulating Labour councillors, including Labour leader Councillor Paul Dimoldenberg, and others on their part in exposing and pursuing the scandal over the past fifteen years?'

Malthouse was not amused by the failure of the settlement agreement with Porter to stem the tide of bad publicity for the Council, so much so that at the next committee meeting to discuss how to spend the Porter money, on 14 July, he accused me of spending 'the last three weeks jumping up and down and accusing us of being crooks'.

Malthouse's petty insults were a minor irritation. My main task was to respond to the incompetent draft Standards Board report. Leonie Cowen had given me some helpful ideas and, on Neale Coleman's suggestion, I contacted Gavin Millar QC for advice. Millar had been a member of the Labour Group from 1985 to 1994 and I had known him since the late 1970s. His family were stalwarts of the St Marylebone Labour Party and his mother, Audrey, is still a very active member. Millar agreed to help without a second's hesitation. He even rebuked me for not contacting him sooner!

A month later, on 1 September, I wrote to the district auditor, Derek Elliott, to tell him that I would be making a formal objection to the Council's accounts for 2003/4. The basis of my objection was that Porter's assets were worth more than the £12.3 million that she offered the City Council, and that the Council agreed to settle for a lesser sum because it wished to dispose of this deeply politically embarrassing issue which it had regarded for the past decade or more as ancient history. I reminded Elliott that all details of why the settlement was agreed and the details of the settlement itself were kept and remain confidential. I also reminded him that Porter's oft-reported wealth was in the region of £60–70 million – considerably more than the £12.3 million accepted by Westminster.

Given that this was the biggest financial scandal in local government history, and the fact that Porter paid less than a third of her surcharge, I also argued that the lack of transparency was of public concern. To underline the seriousness of the objection, I was joined by my Council colleague and barrister Rupert D'Cruz, Peter Bradley, Andrew Dismore MP, Karen Buck and Jonathan Rosenberg, who all made identical objections to the accounts.

Typically, the Council continued its campaign against me, and a letter from Wilson to the Standards Board underlined the anger they felt towards me. On 22 October Wilson wrote:

I am bound to say that, in my own view, some of the issues raised by Councillor Dimoldenberg are now ancient history and are, at best, an unnecessary diversion from the central issues in this case. At worst, they might be said to amount to a cynical attempt by him to distract attention from his own breach of the Code of Conduct by inappropriately and unjustifiably seeking to call into question the integrity of myself and others.

It is clear that in raising these ['Homes for Votes'] issues in his defence of this essentially straightforward complaint, in lodging an objection to the City Council's accounts in respect of the settlement with Dame Shirley Porter and others, and in his dealings with the press, Councillor Dimoldenberg and certain of his political colleagues are determined to do all they can to prevent the City Council from looking forward (rather than back), which, the Appointed Auditor has made clear, is in the public interest.

The Council's tactics did not, however, divert us. On 8 December 2004 D'Cruz, Bradley, Rosenberg and I presented our objection to the accounts case to the district auditor at a three-hour meeting at Westminster City Hall. We pointed out that the Council had failed to contact Porter's former financial adviser, Peter Green, for more than a year after the House of Lords ruled that she should pay the surcharge. We also argued that the Council used the district auditor himself as cover for its failure to recover the money by claiming that he was overseeing the process. Significantly, Elliott admitted that this was an 'unfortunate' description since he had performed no such role.

23

The Standards Board stitch-up

And even if he has been guilty of a technical breach of council guidelines, the success of democracy depends on singular individuals like Cllr Dimoldenberg being prepared to challenge the status quo. When such an individual also has the high moral ground, it seems ludicrous even to suggest that they should be deprived of their democratic mandate. If it is to retain its credibility, the Standards Board will surely kick this complaint into touch. It will be a sad day for democracy if it does not.

Wood & Vale, 19 November 2004

On 1 November 2004 the Standards Board issued its final report and sent it to the president of the Adjudication Panel. The next day the Adjudication Panel told me that the tribunal to consider the Standards Board report would be held on 8 and 9 February 2005. I was given until 2 December to submit representations on the Standards Board report. After consulting Gavin Millar and Leonie Cowen we decided that it would be sensible to ask the Labour Party to get involved and to take over some of the financial responsibility for fighting my case.

Up until now, my case had not been widely known. I had deliberately kept it away from the media, as I was concerned that any attempt by me to tell the media what was happening to me would fall foul of the confidentiality of all the letters I had received from the Standards Board since August 2003. However, the Standards Board had issued its report to the Adjudication Panel and had posted the bare details on its website. It was therefore now in the public domain. But the Standards Board website is hardly required reading for journalists, and the press would need to be directed to it.

That service was provided by the Westminster Conservatives.

The Conservatives tipped off the press because they thought that the story would be very damaging for me and the Labour Group. The reverse turned out to be the case. The local press was totally supportive. For example, on 19 November, the *Wood & Vale* reported:

> Can the Council's campaign against self-confessed whistle blower Cllr Paul Dimoldenberg . . . be seen as anything other than a witch hunt? It is almost as if he is being punished for acting in the public interest. It is certainly fair to say that Cllr Dimoldenberg has never been forgiven by the Tories for joining the whistle blowers who originally exposed the 'Homes for Votes' scandal, in which some of them were embedded.
>
> But now that some of the millions have been recovered, isn't it time for all concerned to move on and bury the hatchet? It will bring no credit to anyone to censure an individual who was clearly motivated by a deep sense of injustice, and who behaved in a manner that would be approved of by the vast majority of taxpayers. Anyone who believes that the councillor's contribution towards the recovery of the money was not motivated by anything other than the greater good, is being churlish in the extreme.

With my case solidly in the public domain I decided to make sure that the story continued to run and I released the details of Peter Rogers's 'signed, undated resignation letter' suggestion. The media, like everyone else, were incredulous. On 26 November the *Wood & Vale* reported: 'Borough boss offered me "disgraceful deal" – Dame Shirley whistleblower reveals secret plan to gag him'. In the editorial comment of the same edition, the paper argued:

> So it transpires that Westminster Council did actually try to 'bury the hatchet' over the alleged leaking of information in the infamous Dame Shirley Porter scandal. But the way it tried to do so was neither honourable nor in keeping with the standards we have a right to expect from a local authority.
>
> The council would drop any action against the maverick councillor

in return for a post dated letter of resignation which could be activated by council chiefs at a time of their own choosing. Not surprisingly, the councillor's party chiefs told the council exactly where to stick their offer. Just imagine the consequences if they had not.

Effectively, a democratically elected councillor would have been serving at the whim of an unelected and, as far as the public is concerned, largely anonymous official. The people who exercised their democratic right by voting Cllr Dimoldenberg into office would have had no idea that their councillor's future depended on the grace and favour of a bureaucrat.

This was a crude attempt to interfere with the democratic process, and it heaps nothing but disdain on the individuals concerned and the council as a whole.

These latest revelations shocked many people, particularly many natural Conservative supporters who could not believe what the Council was doing to me. As a result, I received many calls and letters of support from people across Westminster. I also got to hear snippets of information about the Westminster Conservative Party and Conservative councillors which would not normally come my way.

By far the most significant titbit of information concerned Simon Milton and Robert Davis, who, I was reliably informed, had met Shirley Porter in Tel Aviv in June 2001 – at a time when the whereabouts of her fortune was the subject of an investigation by the Council's forensic accountants and the auditor had given notice of his appeal to the House of Lords. On 6 December I challenged Milton to explain why, as leader of the Council, he had met Porter in Israel. He replied on 14 December and made little of the meeting.

In January 2005 I gave the story to the *Evening Standard*, who prised a very revealing statement out of Milton on 6 January. In it he said:

Shirley Porter is an old friend and a colleague of mine. In June 2001, while attending the wedding in Israel of the daughter of a Council colleague, I and a group of people including Shirley Porter and her husband had dinner in a restaurant in Tel Aviv.

Given my previous friendship with Dame Shirley, I thought it best to have no further contact with her after the House of Lords decision and I also excluded myself from any part in the recovery proceedings in order to avoid any potential perceptions of conflict of interest.

Now that the recovery proceedings are complete and a full and final legal settlement has been arranged between Dame Shirley and the Council, I would be happy to renew my friendship with Dame Shirley should circumstances permit.

The next month, on 1 February, Peter Bradley MP secured an adjournment debate in the House of Commons on the Standards Board. With Karen Buck and Andrew Dismore as support, Bradley launched into a trenchant defence of my actions. He told the Commons:

It is an extraordinary irony, and perhaps an example of the Standards Board at its most confused, that a man of such high integrity, who played so important a role in exposing the worst political corruption in living memory and brought Shirley Porter and her colleagues to justice against all the odds and expectations, should now and over the past eighteen months have faced indictment before the Standards Board – not for any political or personal corruption, and not as a result of a complaint from a member of the public, but as a result of a complaint by Westminster City Council . . . He is arraigned for exercising his judgement and revealing wrongdoing as we and he have done on many previous occasions.

Buck was equally damning of the action that had been taken by the Council against me. She argued:

This is a Council that spawned the largest and costliest gerry-mandering exercise in local government history – one which cost the taxpayer many millions of pounds and caused considerable distress and misery. Many officials and councillors were identified as being complicit. They were aware of wrongdoing but not aware of their duty to stop it. Many of the same councillors involved in the Porter regime remained in office and were responsible for collecting Shirley Porter's £42 million surcharge. A year and half after the case was finally determined in the House of Lords, there were few signs of progress in recovering the debt. Yet an opposition councillor who had exposed the wrongdoing and was wholly committed to the recovery of the £42 million of taxpayers' money finds himself in the dock for attempting to move that recovery forward, even while senior Council officers reveal their own, rather fluid interpretations of both confidentiality and accountability.

Dismore made the telling point that captured the nonsense of my situation:

Councillor Dimoldenberg is charged with bringing Westminster Council into disrepute, which assumes it has a reputation to bring into disrepute in the first place. Looking back over those days, I think that the reputation of Westminster Council is probably the worst in local government, and rightly so.

Bradley, Buck and Dismore's efforts had hit the bull's-eye. At the end of the adjournment debate, Yvette Cooper MP, undersecretary of state at the Office of the Deputy Prime Minister, announced:

The Standards Board will soon be consulting, as part of its complete review of the code [of conduct], on whether and how that part of the code should be amended to deal specifically with the relationship between the code and the Freedom of Information Act and the way in which the public interest should be addressed. It will be asking specifically for views on such issues as whistleblowing, including the case for a public interest defence.

If nothing else, my miserable experience had highlighted a real problem, which the government had, belatedly, recognised and was about to put right.

24

A great victory

> In an unprecedented ruling in a case of this nature, an adjudication panel has agreed to hear a public interest defence by Cllr Dimoldenberg. There are very few restrictions in any form of government that should outweigh the public interest. This, clearly, wasn't one of them. Cllr Dimoldenberg's war is not yet over but he has won an important battle, not just for his own sake, but on behalf of conscientious public representatives everywhere.
>
> *Wood & Vale*, 11 February 2005

In the run-up to the Adjudication Panel tribunal on 8 February 2005, Gavin Millar had successfully persuaded the three-member tribunal – Steve Wells, Richard Tyndall and Keith Stevens – to allow us to present arguments on mounting a public interest defence. Millar is a Human Rights Act specialist and he was totally confident that we had the law on our side. His arguments were no doubt helped by Yvette Cooper's recent statement in the House of Commons.

A packed public gallery in the basement conference suite at the Strand Palace Hotel heard Millar make a convincing argument to the case tribunal. It was terrific to see so many supporters who had given up their time to be there. Millar spoke for over two hours. Referring to the *Washington Post* reporters who broke the Watergate scandal in the 1970s, he told the tribunal: 'You do not need to be Woodward and Bernstein to see that disclosure was in the public interest in this case.' Afterwards I told him how impressive he had been. He brushed the praise aside. 'I know this stuff backwards,' he said. 'I've made these points so many times, I could recite it all.' As we broke for lunch, Millar's self-deprecating remarks were enormously reassuring.

My confidence in Millar was spot on. After hearing arguments from the Standards Board's counsel, Jacques Algazy, the case tribunal decided that I was entitled to mount a public interest defence and set the date for the further three-day hearing for 18 May. And on 17 February, the Standards Board finally launched its comprehensive review of the Code of Conduct. Among the areas considered by the review was 'Whistleblowing – should there be an explicit public interest defence for people disclosing confidential information?'

Stung by its humiliating defeat, the Standards Board changed its counsel. On 11 February the board's solicitor, Storm Westmaas, informed Gerald Shamash, the Labour Party's solicitor, who had taken over from Cowen, that Antony White QC of Matrix Chambers had been instructed by the Standards Board. White was a far more experienced barrister than Algazy. It was clear that if Millar could recite all the relevant cases, then White could probably do the same with his chosen legal texts. White, also, was not going to be outgunned. He brought along an experienced 'junior', Heather Rogers, who had recently represented the BBC's Andrew Gilligan at the Hutton inquiry. White, no doubt, wanted to be able to call on Rogers's knowledge of the BBC in formulating his attack on any evidence submitted by Andy Hosken and the *Today* programme.

The Westminster Conservatives, too, were mightily upset by the Adjudication Panel's ruling in my favour. Once again the attack was led by Kit Malthouse, who claimed that I had 'very nearly cost us the whole settlement [£12.3 million] by tipping off Dame Shirley about what we were doing. The man took information and passed it on for political advantage. The idea that he was doing anything other than for naked political ambition is laughable' (*Wood & Vale*, 18 February 2005). Malthouse also denied that the Council had been dragging its feet until the *Today* programme was broadcast. 'We had very forensic work going on into people's computers and hard disks,' he said, but forgot to add that all that started in July 2003, after the BBC broadcasts.

Of course, as we now know, before the *Today* programme, Council officers were actively considering recommending Conservative councillors to discontinue the search for Porter's money. Colin Wilson had also already instructed Stephenson Harwood to put the most junior member of staff on the case to reduce the Council's costs. Dithering was too kind a word to describe the Council's defeatist approach before we put a rocket up them.

The following week events took another bizarre twist when the Council provided me with details of the Porter settlement but, in the same breath, told me that I could not use the information in my defence because of the confidentiality deal that the Council had struck with Porter. More bizarre still, I was forbidden to even show the papers to my legal advisers, Millar and Shamash. I was now in the crazy situation where the Council that had lodged the complaint against me was using confidentiality clauses to hamper my defence. And, of course, if I released any of that information during the course of my defence the Council would be waiting eagerly to lodge another complaint against me for breaching the Code of Conduct. They must have been having a good laugh at City Hall.

In the period between February and May I worked hard to persuade friends and colleagues to write letters of support to the Adjudication Panel and to the local press. I wanted the under-siege Standards Board and Adjudication Panel to be aware that a decision to ban or suspend me would not be popular amongst MPs and councillors, in particular. I also organised a petition and my Labour Group colleagues Barrie Taylor and Guthrie McKie ran a fund-raising campaign to pay for the legal fees. The response to all these requests for help was extraordinary. Letters were sent in my support from political friends in London and wider afield; constituents in Queen's Park wrote in support as did friends from the cemeteries and Dolphin Square campaigns. Cheques arrived from Labour Groups in all parts of the UK, as well as from Labour Party members in Westminster.

So, by the time the second Adjudication Panel hearing started on 18 May 2005, this time at the Aeonian Centre, off Tottenham Court Road, I was in good spirits. I was determined to put up a very robust defence. I was also absolutely determined that I would not go quietly. Millar was in top form. He opened by criticising the failure of the Standards Board to call either Peter Rogers, John Fordham or Wilson as witnesses, thereby depriving us of the opportunity to cross-examine them. He argued that my actions were driven by a desire 'to ensure that story had the public momentum to push the Council into doing something to collect the money Porter owed'. He also explained that I believed that 'Council officers had fobbed off Labour colleagues' who had asked about progress and that I 'did not believe that the Audit Commission would intervene successfully if [I] took the information to them'.

In the afternoon I was in the witness box for almost three hours. I told the Adjudication Panel that the Council was more interested in silencing me than recovering the money owed by Porter. I referred the panel to the note of the meeting held on 30 June 2003, just prior to when I handed over the various emails linking John Porter's money with that of his mother. That meeting included Council officers and the Audit Commission. Far from discussing the recovery of the Porter money, I reminded the Adjudication Panel that 'it was all about how we can kill the story, because it was politically embarrassing to them'.

Under cross-examination from White I told the Adjudication Panel that I took my lead from the district auditor's call for councillors to 'speak up' when they believed something wrong was happening. Grandly, I invoked Edmund Burke's ringing phrase: 'All that is needed for evil to triumph is for good men to do nothing.' During questioning I told the panel:

> I was keen to ensure that Mr Hosken had the full picture so that he could write a totally accurate piece for the BBC. Giving partial information could have led him down a blind alley, resulting in inaccurate conclusions or him writing a wrong story that might put the quest for Porter's £42 million into question. I did not want this to happen. I fervently wanted the Council to collect that £42 million, not least because of the pressing housing problems that the money could be used for.

I repeated my central belief that the £12.3 million settlement would not have been offered by Porter if the BBC had not run the story. 'I do not believe that it would have happened if the BBC had not done such a good programme setting out all the facts,' I argued.

When asked why I did not own up to leaking the confidential Council material when initially asked, I accepted my mistake. I confessed: 'My policy was one of denial. I should have said: "Get lost, I have done nothing wrong." But when you are threatened you don't always do what's in your best interests.'

I made it very clear that I believed that the Council had been motivated by 'pure personal spite' in taking action against me: 'I knew people would come after me and they would want to take revenge for me exposing their failings. The fact they did come after me, making a complaint just weeks later, showed my instincts were correct.'

I ended my evidence by expressing pride that my actions forced the Council to speed up its action to recover the money Porter owed. Finally, I paid tribute to the team of which I was part, and repeated Harry S. Truman's famous phrase, 'There's no limit on what you can achieve if no one minds who gets the credit'. That was the way in which we operated and I will always believe that we had achieved a great deal.

The next day, it was Andy Hosken's turn to face a grilling from White. Hosken was very firm and explained his anger at being duped by Stephenson Harwood into giving them information which was used immediately by the Council to make the complaint about me to the Standards Board. He told the Adjudication Panel:

> They were snooping around the BBC looking for information and had quite wrongly used the information to finger Councillor Dimoldenberg as a source. That was absolutely outrageous when we were trying to help them resolve one the greatest acts of misbehaviour in local government. I thought Ms Griffiths [of Stephenson Harwood] was there to gather information which may assist her company recover monies from Dame Shirley, not to pry on behalf of Westminster Council and attempt to discover my sources of information. I would not have given documents to Stephenson Harwood if I knew they could be used for anything other than to assist the recovery efforts.

Hosken made a public apology to me for what he described as an 'unforgivable breach' of the agreement that we made that the information I gave him would be used only as deep background. He then responded to White's probing in robust fashion. He told the Adjudication Panel: 'We were acting in the public interest. Within ten days John Porter had action taken against him and Peter Green's computers were taken away, and in the end the Council got a settlement of £12.3 million.'

When asked about the confidential information I had given him, Hosken admitted: 'Technically I should not have had this information. I should not have known there were gagging orders.' But he added: 'I get secret information all the time and there was no more a case for working in the public interest than this.'

Throughout the three-day panel hearing the public gallery was regularly full of supporters, some for just an hour or two, but a few gluttons for punishment, such as Audrey Millar, Barbara Grahame, Sharan Tabari, Tony Mothersdale, Eileen Sheppard, Jo Mahoney and Guthrie McKie, were there for practically the whole time. I owe them all a huge debt of gratitude. We all had to wait for over a day – from mid-afternoon on Thursday 19 May to 4.00 p.m. on Friday 20 May – for a decision. When the decision came it was a great victory.

The Adjudication Panel dismissed the charge that I had brought the Council into disrepute and decided that no action was merited by what was no more than a technical breach of the Code of Conduct. Announcing the decision, the case tribunal chairman, Steve Wells, said: 'No sanction should be imposed on you. We noted in particular that there was no financial gain or political kudos. Neither was there any damage caused to Westminster City Council in its recovery proceedings.' The Adjudication Panel added that the Council's recovery process 'might well have been assisted' by my action. It also noted 'the large number of letters from of support from MPs, councillors, residents and others'.

What a victory!

I had spent the Friday morning drafting two different press statements, starting with one responding to a negative decision. Thankfully, that draft ended up in the waste paper basket and, later that day, I was able to claim: 'This is a great day for local government, for democracy and for the freedom of the press.'

The Council's response was typically churlish. On 24 May it issued a press statement not only claiming that it had secured a victory, but also attacking the decision to take no action against me:

> The Panel has decided that Councillor Dimoldenberg was indeed in breach of the Members Code of Conduct, thus vindicating the Chief Executive's decision to refer the matter to the Standards Board. The Panel has decided, in this case, that no sanction should be imposed, although clearly there will be significant implications for the conduct of local authority business generally if this decision is seen by others as a signal that breaches of confidence will go unpunished.

I was incensed by the Council's continued mean-minded approach, and any thought of putting the past behind me and moving on quickly went by the wayside. I wrote a letter to the *Wood & Vale* which expressed my anger with the Council and the Standards Board:

> Why did the Standards Board need two highly paid barristers – Antony White and Heather Rogers – to prosecute their case against me? Were they so unsure of their case that one barrister was not enough? How much did this latest Standards Board fiasco cost the taxpayer? Will there be an inquiry?
>
> And what of the Westminster Chief Executive and the Council's Monitoring Officer? Are they going to take any responsibility for what must rank as one of the most spectacular errors of judgment of recent times? (*Wood & Vale*, 27 May 2005)

Having got that off my chest, my immediate concerns were more practical. How was I going to pay the legal bills, which had come in at over £45,000? The financial appeal had raised around £26,000 but there was still a £19,000 hole. I knew that back in 1998 the Council reimbursed three Conservative councillors, Alex Segal, Barry Legg and Miles Young, a combined total of over £240,000 for the legal fees they incurred in fighting the district auditor. So on 3 June I wrote to the Council making a request for the reimbursement of half of my legal fees on the grounds that one of the two charges against me had been thrown out.

I was sure that the Council's Conservative-dominated Standards Committee would not agree to my request. However, Gavin Millar made it clear that the Council had the legal powers to make the payment. Unsurprisingly, the Council dragged things out through a combination of incompetence and bloody-mindedness and the request was not considered properly until 23 November, almost six months later. As I expected, the Conservatives threw out my request, despite the fact that in 1998 they had paid three of their colleagues. But, according to Conservative councillors, that was different. So they got nearly a quarter of a million pounds and I got nothing. Yes, even in 2005, the Westminster Conservatives were still at it!

In the meantime, the district auditor, Derek Elliott, decided on 11 August to 'recuse himself' (i.e. stand down) from hearing our objection into the Council's 2003/4 accounts. He told us: 'I have now formed the view that the extent of my involvement in this highly exceptional case and the way in which this was recorded in various documents is such that a fair-minded and informed observer could conclude that there is a real possibility of the appearance of bias.' He was then replaced by the new Westminster district auditor, Les Kidner.

And in September the case against Cliff Stanford and George Liddell came to court. On the fourteenth they were both cleared of conspiring to blackmail Shirley Porter and her son John. However, they both admitted unauthorised interception of emails and both were given six-month suspended sentences. Stanford was fined £20,000, but, essentially, the suspended sentences were an acknowledgement that their offence was purely technical. After all, their information had proved crucial to cracking the code to Porter's millions.

Finally, on 1 January 2006, Simon Milton was awarded a knighthood in the New Year's Honours list, for his 'services to local government'. 'It represents a wonderful endorsement for everything we have achieved at Westminster,' Sir Simon claimed. As they say, you couldn't make it up.

25

Reflections

After 15 long years, the Westminster gerrymandering scandal seems to be over. Much of the credit should go to the former district auditor John Magill. For a long while the saga took over his life. Despite his victory, few expected the money to be recovered. A lot of people deserve credit. But few in truth could match Magill for persistence and determination.

Accountancy Age, 29 April 2004

So, after over twenty years, what do the Westminster scandals amount to and what have I learned from it all?

First, I learned the hard way that opposition is hugely important but it is not easy. Holding the executive to account is very difficult. You have to take every opportunity and be prepared to be difficult and unpopular. The majority party and the people who serve it have a vested interest in keeping you in the dark about anything that might embarrass them. You have to probe and constantly ask questions. The new cabinet/scrutiny arrangements simply do not work. Councils, not just Westminster, are very good at scrutinising the NHS, Royal Mail, the water companies and anybody else. But, they find it very difficult to scrutinise themselves. It's all too politically embarrassing. So, three cheers for the Freedom of Information Act, which has made it difficult for the bureaucracy to clam up completely. You still, however, have to know what questions to ask. So helpful leaks from insiders will still be a very important element of the democratic process.

Second, proving allegations of wrongdoing against the rich and powerful is hard work. We had a tough job to persuade people of the scale of the Conservatives' wrongdoing. Because it was

Westminster, many people's first instinct was to believe that everything that went on at City Hall was totally above board; that scandals were confined to the Lambeths and Hackneys of this world. Even when we produced the evidence we had an uphill struggle to get the authorities to take action. John Magill's initial reaction to our allegations was to believe the fiction, lies and half-truths he was told by Council officers. Every step of the way it was up to us to produce the evidence that would persuade the authorities to investigate.

Third, you need teamwork and an array of skills to do opposition well. We were incredibly lucky at Westminster. The Labour Group was full of talent and brain power – as evidenced by the high-powered jobs that Neale Coleman, Karen Buck, Andrew Dismore, Peter Bradley and David Pitt-Watson went on to do. We were blessed with two fantastic support staff, Margaret Malcolm between 1986 and 1990 and Veronica Mockler from 1990 onwards. They dealt with the masses of individual casework which was generated, gathered and maintained the growing amount of information we needed, and kept the office working effectively. The Conservatives had thousands of staff at their beck and call. We could not have done it without Margaret and Veronica. Thankfully, there were very few egos around. We shared jobs and played to people's strengths. We had no rows about who should get the kudos for blowing the whistle. We shared the plaudits. And when the votes went against us – as they did spectacularly in 1990 – we shared the grief and there were no recriminations.

Fourth, you need to be organised to be effective. Unlocking both the 15p cemeteries and the 'Homes for Votes' scandals involved putting together detailed chronologies of events. The more we dug, the more information we found. Gradually, these small fragments built up into the big picture. Doing this required access to all kinds of information, much of it held by the Council.

Fifth, and leading on from the previous point, our experience at Westminster was an example of how those in power manipulate information, particularly 'confidential' information, to keep their grip on power and prevent their opponents from holding them to account. Westminster's use of the 'confidential' label was a classic way of keeping politically embarrassing information secret. Until, that is, it suits them to make it public for their own political purposes.

Of course, this is not just confined to the Conservatives. The former Labour Prime Minister Jim Callaghan famously shared with the Franks committee his old ministerial adage of 'I brief, you leak' – a very succinct summary of how those in power operate. More recently, Peter Hyman, a former Downing Street speechwriter, recalls his discussions with Alastair Campbell following their vetting interviews with Special Branch in 1997:

'Would you ever hand over government information to the press?' the security man asked.

'Yes,' Alastair replied. 'Tony pays me to do so.'

(*One out of Ten*, Vintage, 2005)

Sixth, being a whistleblower is not to be undertaken on your own. You need a great deal of support to get through everything that is hurled at you by a powerful organisation stung at being exposed very publicly in the national media. I was lucky. I had a very supportive family and a great set of colleagues who rallied round and offered help, advice and reassurance. Being a whistle-blower is not just about passing information about wrongdoing to the authorities and hoping that they will do something about it. It is also about protecting yourself against the attacks you will get from those who have a lot to lose from what you have revealed.

Finally, holding decision-makers to account is a vital role in a democracy – whether it be the Cabinet or the town hall. This is even more so in a council such as Westminster, where a change of political control is no more than theoretical. Without the Westminster Whistleblowers, the biggest scandal in local government history would never have been uncovered. Working closely with the media was the only way that this could be achieved. A free press and determined, skilful journalists made everything possible. As Lord Scott remarked in his 2001 House of Lords judgment:

When detected and exposed it must be expected, or at least it must be hoped for, that political corruption will receive its just deserts at the polls. Detection and exposure is, however, often difficult and, where it happens, is usually attributable to determined efforts by political opponents or by investigative journalists or by both in tandem.

Scott's perceptive comments crystallise the importance of the Westminster Whistleblowers in the annals of local government history. All of those involved are entitled to feel a tremendous pride in their unique achievements.

Index